ATHEIST TO CATHOLIC

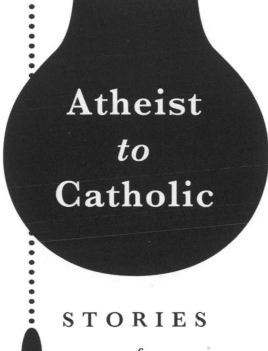

Atheist *to* Catholic

STORIES *of* CONVERSION

REBECCA VITZ CHERICO

editor

SERVANT BOOKS

PUBLISHED BY ST. ANTHONY MESSENGER PRESS
CINCINNATI, OHIO

Unless otherwise noted, Scripture passages have been taken from the *Revised Standard Version*, Catholic edition. Copyright 1946, 1952, 1971 by the Division of Christian Education of the National Council of Churches of Christ in the USA. Used by permission. All rights reserved. The title for Mattie Berhang's story and other passages marked *NAB* are from the *New American Bible*. Scripture texts in this work marked *NAB* are taken from the *New American Bible with Revised New Testament and Revised Psalms* © 1991, 1986, 1970 Confraternity of Christian Doctrine, Washington, D.C. and are used by permission of the copyright owner. All Rights Reserved. No part of the *New American Bible* may be reproduced in any form without permission in writing from the copyright owner. Passages marked *KJV* are from the King James Version.

ISBN 978-0-86716-957-7

LIBRARY OF CONGRESS CATALOGING-IN-PUBLICATION DATA
Atheist to Catholic : stories of conversion / edited by Rebecca Vitz Cherico.
p. cm.
Includes bibliographical references.
ISBN 978-0-86716-957-7 (alk. paper)
1. Catholic converts—United States—Biography. 2. Atheists—United States—Biography. I. Cherico, Rebecca Vitz.
BX4668.A1A85 2011
282'.730922—dc22
[B]
2011001385

Published by Servant Books, an imprint of St. Anthony Messenger Press.
28 W. Liberty St.
Cincinnati, OH 45202
www.AmericanCatholic.org
www.ServantBooks.org

Printed in the United States of America.

Printed on acid-free paper.

11 12 13 14 15   5 4 3 2 1

CONTENTS

———

PREFACE

W hen I was a freshman in high school, I had an intelligent and inspired young theology teacher. Michael Johanek was responsible for the "world religions" component of our school's curriculum, and he took the responsibility seriously. He started from the beginning of human history and spoke of primitive man and woman's—"Stosh and Olga's"— search for truth and meaning. After covering the major faiths of the world, Mr. Johanek concluded the school year with secularism, with its basic tenets and rites of passage.

I am deeply grateful for the many insights that Mr. Johanek passed on to us and particularly for his presentation of the religion of the contemporary world. Secularism is not the same as atheism, of course, but adherents to atheistic positions often equate the two, ignoring the fact that their atheism is, in many ways, a belief system. As with any faith, its adherents may be loath to relinquish beliefs that they have subscribed to for a long time. And as happens with any commonly accepted cultural practice, many atheists do not even realize the assumptions they make about the world and themselves.

A number of prominent atheists have recently published works in which they attempt to proselytize. Radical misrepresentations of religious belief and believers seem to bother them very little. This is especially interesting when we consider that these public atheists usually claim that their position is the more reasonable one, the one supported by "the evidence."

The stories that follow will seriously challenge that position. Many people in this book—and people who knew them—were almost shocked by their turn to faith. Their stories are a public witness to the fact that the truth is deeper and grander than many suppose, and the Church's truth is accessible to everyone, not just those who have been exposed to it from birth.

Both of my parents are converts (my father's story is included here), and I am a semi-convert to Catholicism (I was baptized Episcopalian and entered the Church with my First Communion). Given my familiarity with conversion, it is curious to me how strange it often appears to others. "Oh, really?" people will say when that learning my parents *became* Catholic. "How bizarre," or, "Why would anyone ever do that?" appear to be the subtext to their commentary. But converts to Catholicism are not as rare as our popular culture leads us to think.

Perhaps more importantly, converts have good reasons for what they have done, and their conversions can enlighten all our paths. Stories of conversion function as a sort of chiaroscuro for the rest of us; they show in strong relief the dramas that we all face, illuminating the bright points and letting the darkness recede into the background.

I have taught a freshman seminar at Villanova University for a number of years that focuses on some of the great books of Western civilization. Since Villanova is an Augustinian college, we are required to teach a work of Augustine; I always choose his *Confessions.* In teaching that great work (quoted by one of our converts in this volume), I have had the good fortune of discussing conversion with many students. Few of them are converts, and most of them know few religious converts, so they do not relate in an obvious or immediate way to Augustine's religious journey. And yet they were familiar with many of the conflicts and challenges Augustine experienced. While far from his life circumstances, they identify very strongly with many of the trials he faced personally and intellectually.

The search for truth and meaning is something that characterizes our very humanity; the convert's story is a clear and satisfying depiction of the quest that we all are engaged in. Reading and rereading Augustine's story also reminds me how long the process of conversion can take: While a convert may remember a given and dramatic moment (like Augustine's "*Tolle, lege*" scene), there can be many small but decisive moments leading up to that point. For those of us who do not have a single "aha" moment in the history of our lives and our faith, recognizing the smaller moments is central to following God's process of leading us more fully to him. Conversion is never over, neither for the convert nor for the rest of us.

I would dare to say that virtually all adult Catholics are converts in some sense: All those who have stayed Catholic have done so *against* the current of our popular culture. In this sense converts' stories clarify the choices and decisions that face all of us. There can be a temptation for cradle Catholics with doubts about their faith to believe that any continued interest in God is the psychological residue of having been raised a certain way. Hearing stories about people with no such residue who, nevertheless, faced the same questions and came to the faith can help us realize that Christ and the Church answer our *human* needs.

A compelling thing I notice in these stories is the number of times a friend or acquaintance plays a critical role. Often it begins casually: a conversation at a party or in class, someone seen going to Mass, or uttering a quick prayer. The ways in which friends enter a person's life and change it forever are many and varied, just like the people themselves. Sometimes those friends are not even living: They are authors whose words reach across time and space to a person's mind and heart.

I believe that it is essential for us to realize that we may be called to be that decisive person on someone's road to faith. We do not know when and how the Lord will call us (even unwittingly) to intervene, but we can be ready and willing to do so. No one is ever truly lost to God, and we should never give up hope (or prayer) that someone we love will surprise us by hearing and following the Lord's call.

Finally, conversion stories remind me of the tremendous importance and power of prayer. Most of the converts in this volume mention prayers—even half-uttered ones—that were answered in dramatic and life-altering ways.

When converts review their lives and their conversions, they sometimes end up rethinking their lives on many levels.

For some it is even difficult to feel that they ever were "complete" atheists, because they have become aware of God's hand in their lives from the very beginning. On a similar note, I have noticed that many converts describe their conversion experience as "coming home," even when they had no Catholic background, not even culturally. It is a reminder of the fact that we are made by him and for him: We recognize that we are where we belong when we get there.

In preparing this volume, I have had the great privilege and blessing to be in touch with a large number of converts. When I first started reading people's stories, I often had the impression that there was something missing: People's accounts of their conversion seemed to show mysterious lacunae or gaps. But as I read more and more, I realized that there was nothing missing in the stories themselves; rather something bigger and more mysterious was acting in certain moments of the person's life, something that the writer did not know how to explain or account for. I have since learned to relish those gaps, to look for them as the sign of the Spirit's presence in people's lives.

I have been personally inspired by all the stories in this volume, inspired by the honesty and courage people have shown in telling about themselves, often revealing failings and limitations that people usually seek to conceal. I have also been impressed by the determination people displayed in following the truth.

This is a book of seekers who ended up someplace they never intended to go; and yet they went there, even if it was inconvenient, awkward, or strange. Their commitment to following God's prompting is a tremendous witness. Their courage and zeal in going where the truth led them are matched by the amazing way we see God intervene in situations that appear impossible. Where we have the strength to leave even a little opening, God rushes in.

——

CHAPTER ONE

Following Logic to Its Surprising Conclusions
John C. Wright

John C. Wright is a newspaperman and editor, attorney, philoso-
pher, and writer of science fiction novels, the most famous of which,
Orphans of Chaos, *was nominated for a Nebula Award in 2006.*
In appearance he is bespectacled, bewhiskered, not so much tall as
huge, and his affectations include a pocket watch, a low-crowned,
broad-brimmed black hat, and a walking stick with the dullest of
sword blades hidden inside. He is the father of four—Orville,
Roland, Juss, and Eve—and lives in fairy tale–like happiness with
his wife, Jagi, in the Commonwealth of Virginia.

Here John tells of the odd circumstances surrounding his conver-
sion to the faith of Christ.

My conversion was in two parts: a natural part and a
supernatural part. Here is the natural part:

First, over a period of two years, my hatred toward
Christianity eroded due to my philosophical inquiries. Rest
assured, I take the logical process of philosophy very seriously, and I am impatient with anyone who is not a rigorous

and trained thinker. Reason is the tool men use to determine if their statements about reality are valid; there is no other. Those who do not or cannot reason are little better than slaves, because their lives are controlled by the ideas of other men, ideas they have not examined.

To my surprise and alarm, I found that, step by step, logic drove me to conclusions no modern philosophy shared but only this ancient and (as I saw it then) corrupt and superstitious foolery called the Church. Each time I followed an argument fearlessly, it led me, one remorselessly rational step at a time, to a position the church had been maintaining for more than a thousand years. That haunted me.

Second, I began to notice how shallow, either simply optimistic or simply pessimistic, other philosophies and views of life are. The public conduct of my fellow atheists was so lacking in sobriety and gravity that I began to wonder why, if we atheists had a hammerlock on truth, so much of what we said was pointless or naive. Some sounded as innocent of any notion of what real human life was like as the man from Mars who has never met human beings or even heard clear rumors of them. I remember listening to a fellow atheist telling me how wonderful the world would be once religion was swept into the dustbin of history, and I realized the chap knew nothing about history. If atheism solved all human woe, then the Soviet Union would have been an empire of joy and dancing bunnies instead of a land of corpses.

Then I would read something written by Christian men of letters—Tolkien, Lewis, or G.K. Chesterton—and see a solid understanding of the joys and woes of human life. They were mature men. I would look at the rigorous logic of

St. Thomas Aquinas, the complexity and thoroughness of his reasoning, and compare that to the scattered and mentally incoherent sentimentality of some poseur like Nietzsche or Sartre. I can tell the difference between a rigorous argument and shrill psychological flatulence. I can see the difference between a giant and a dwarf.

My wife is a Christian and is extraordinarily patient, logical, and philosophical. For years I would challenge and condemn her beliefs, battering the structure of her conclusions with every argument, analogy, and evidence I could bring to bear. (I am a very argumentative man, and I am as fell and subtle as a serpent in debate.) All my arts failed against her.

I discovered that the death sentence under which all life suffers no longer applied to me. The governor, so to speak, had phoned.

At last I was forced to conclude that, like non-Euclidian geometry, my wife's worldview logically followed from its axioms (although the axioms were radically mystical, and I rejected them with contempt). Her persistence compared favorably to the behavior of my fellow atheists, most of whom cannot utter any argument more mentally alert than a silly *ad hominem* attack. Once again I saw that I was confronting a mature and serious worldview, not merely a tissue of fables and superstitions.

Third, a friend asked me what evidence, if any, would be sufficient to convince me that the supernatural existed. This question stumped me. My philosophy at the time excluded the contemplation of the supernatural axiomatically; by definition (my definition) even the word *supernatural* was a contradiction in terms. Logic then said that, if my conclusions

were definitional, they were circular. I was assuming the conclusion of the subject matter in dispute.

Now, my philosophy at the time was as rigorous and exact
as thirty-five years of study could make it. (I started philosophy when I was seven.) This meant there was no point for
reasonable doubt in the foundational structure of my
axioms, definitions, and common notions. Even if God
existed and manifested himself to me, my philosophy would
force me to reject the evidence of my senses and dismiss any
manifestations as coincidence, hallucination, or dream.
Under this hypothetical my philosophy would force me to
an exactly wrong conclusion due to structural errors of
assumption.

A philosopher (and I mean a serious and manly philosopher, not a sophomoric boy) does not use philosophy to
flinch away from truth or hide from it. A philosophy com-
posed of structural false-to-facts assumptions is insupport-
able. A philosopher goes where the truth leads and has no
patience with mere emotion.

But it was impossible, logically impossible, that I should
ever believe in such nonsense as the supernatural. It would
take a miracle to get me to believe in miracles. So I prayed.

> Dear God,
> I know (because I can prove it with the certainty
> that a geometer can prove opposite angles are
> equal) that you do not exist. Nonetheless, as a
> scholar I am forced to entertain the hypothetical
> possibility that I am mistaken. So just in case I am
> mistaken, please reveal yourself to me in some fash-
> ion that will prove your case.

If you do not answer, I can safely assume that either you do not care whether I believe in you or you have no power to produce evidence to persuade me. The former argues you are not beneficent, the latter not omnipotent—in either case, unworthy of worship. If you do not exist, this prayer is merely words in the air, and I lose nothing but a bit of my dignity.

Thanking you in advance for your kind cooperation in this matter,

John Wright

I had a heart attack two days later. God obviously has a sense of humor as well as a sense of timing.

Now for the supernatural part:

My wife called someone from her church, which is of a denomination that practices healing through prayer. My wife read a passage from the denomination's writings, and the pain vanished. If this was a coincidence, then, by heaven, I could use more coincidences like that in my life.

Feeling fit, I nonetheless went to the hospital to find out what had happened to me. The diagnosis was grave, and a quintuple bypass surgery was ordered. So I was in the hospital for a few days.

Those were the happiest days of my life. A sense of peace and confidence, a peace that passes all understanding, like a field of energy, entered my body. I grew aware of a spiritual dimension of reality of which I had hitherto been unaware. It was like a man born blind suddenly receiving sight.

The truth to which my lifetime as a philosopher had been devoted turned out to be a living thing. It turned and looked at me. Something from beyond the reach of time and space, more fundamental than reality, reached across the universe and broke into my soul and changed me. This was not a case of defense and prosecution laying out evidence for my reason to pick through: I was altered down to the root of my being. It was like falling in love. If you have not been in love, I cannot explain it. If you have, you will raise a glass with me in toast.

Naturally I was overjoyed. First, I discovered that the death sentence under which all life suffers no longer applied to me. The governor, so to speak, had phoned. Second, imagine how puffed up with pride you'd be to find out you were the son of Caesar, and all the empire would be yours. How much more then to find out you were the child of God!

I was also able to perform, for the first time in my life, the act that I had studied philosophy all my life to perform, which is to put aside all fear of death. The Roman Stoics, whom I so admire, speak volumes about this philosophical fortitude. But their lessons could not teach me this virtue. The blessing of the Holy Spirit could and did impart it to me, as a gift. So the thing I'd been seeking my whole life was now mine. Then, just to make sure I was flooded with evidence, I received three visions, like Scrooge being visited by three ghosts. I was not drugged or semiconscious; I was perfectly alert and in my right wits. It was not a dream: I have had dreams every night of my life; I know what a dream is. It was not a hallucination: I know someone who suffers from hallucinations, and I know the signs; those signs were not present here.

Then, just to make it even surer, I had a religious experience. Separate from the visions, this took place several days after my release from the hospital, when my health was moderately good. I was not taking any painkillers, by the way, because I found that prayer could banish pain in moments.

During this experience I became aware of the origin of all thought, the underlying oneness of the universe, the nature of time: The paradox of determinism and free will was resolved for me. I saw and experienced part of the workings of a mind infinitely superior to mine, a mind able to count every atom in the universe, filled with paternal love and jovial good humor. The cosmos created by the thought of this mind was as intricate as a symphony, with themes and reflections repeating themselves forward and backward through time. I saw the illusionary nature of pain and the logical impossibility of death.

Now, as far as these experiences go, they are not unique. They are not even unusual. More people have had religious experiences than have seen the far side of the moon. Dogmas disagree, but mystics are strangely (I am tempted to say, mystically) in agreement. The things I was shown have echoes in both pagan and Christian traditions, both Eastern and Western (although, with apologies to my pagan friends, I see that Christianity is the clearest expression of these themes and also has a logical and ethical character other religious expressions lack).

Further, the worldview implied by taking this vision seriously (1) gives supernatural sanction to conclusions only painfully reached by logic, (2) supports and justifies a mature rather than simplistic worldview, and (3) fits in with the majority traditions not merely of the West but also, in a limited way, of the East.

As a side issue, the solution of various philosophical conundrums—like the problem of the one and the many, mind-body duality, determinism and indeterminism, and so on—is an added benefit. I follow the panentheist idealism of Bishop Berkeley (the belief that God is real and interpenetrates all of reality and beyond); and no, Mr. Johnson does not refute him merely by kicking a stone.

From that time to this, I have had prayers answered and seen miracles: Each individually could be explained away as a coincidence by a skeptic but not taken as a whole. From that time to this, I continue to be aware of the Holy Spirit within me, like feeling a heartbeat. It is a primary impression coming not through the medium of the senses: an intuitive axiom, like the knowledge of one's own being.

It would not be rational for me to doubt something of which I am aware on a primary and fundamental level. Occam's razor (the principle that the simplest solution is usually the correct one) cuts out hallucination or dream as a likely explanation for my experiences. In order to fit these experiences into an atheistic framework, I would have to resort to endless ad hoc explanations: This lacks the elegance of geometers and the parsimony of philosophers. I would also have to assume all the great thinkers of history were fools. While I was perfectly content to support this belief back in my days as an atheist, this is a flattering conceit difficult to maintain seriously.

On a pragmatic level, I am somewhat more useful to my fellowman than before and certainly more charitable. If it is a daydream, why wake me up? My neighbors will not thank you if I stop believing in the mystical brotherhood of man. Besides, the atheist's non-god is not going to send me to non-hell for my lapse of non-faith if it should turn out that I am mistaken.

CHAPTER TWO

Finding the Fingerprints of God
Jennifer Fulwiler

Jennifer Fulwiler is a writer as well as the director of chaos manage-ment for her growing family, which currently includes four children under the age of seven. Her writing has been published in over a dozen publications, including National Lampoon, Inside Catholic, This Rock, Envoy, *and* Our Sunday Visitor, *and she's been featured on national radio networks like Sirius Radio and Relevant Radio. She's also a columnist for* Envoy *magazine and a regular guest on EWTN Radio's* SonRise Morning Show.

In 2007 Jennifer became Catholic after a life of atheism. She blogs about faith, conversion, and the joy of the Catholic life at ConversionDiary.com.

"We got the test results," the hematologist said, walking into the stark examining room where I sat with my aching leg propped on a stool. I was pregnant with my second child. A severe pain in my right calf had landed me in the emergency room only days before, and I had been diagnosed with a deep vein thrombosis, a life-threatening blood clot.

10

"The clot wasn't an isolated incident," the doctor continued. "You have a genetic clotting disorder that makes pregnancy very dangerous for you." He went on to explain that the medication that would be used postpartum to treat the clot was so dangerous for pregnancy that I'd need to use multiple forms of contraception while on it, and I shouldn't have any more children.

"Is there a problem?" he asked when he saw my stunned reaction. There was, but I couldn't bring myself to tell him what it was.

The problem was that I was considering converting to Catholicism after a life of atheism, and the Catholic Church taught that the use of artificial contraception was wrong. After a year of intensive research, I felt certain that the church was correct on these matters. But now my own health was at stake, and I faced the alluring option of taking the easy path by using contraception. Mortified at the idea of being perceived as a "religious person," I told the doctor that I wanted to continue our conversation about my treatment options at our next appointment, later in the week. That gave me three days to consider how serious I was about converting.

My father was an atheist. I'm not as certain about my mom's beliefs; if there's a word for "figuring that if God exists you'll be fine because you're a good person, but finding religious stuff too uninteresting to think about," that's what she was. I don't know if my parents intended to raise me as an atheist. Perhaps they thought that they wouldn't address the topic of religion at all, but we lived in the Bible Belt, which put me on the receiving end of many evangelization efforts. When I started asking my parents questions like whether hell was in the United States, which I wanted to know because friends at school said our family would be spending a lot of time there, my atheistic education began.

More than just detailing the logical flaws in our Christian neighbors' belief system and warning about the intellectual perils of buying into religion, my father instilled in me a strong desire to question assumptions. "Never believe something just because someone else says it's true, or because it makes you feel good, or because you want it to be true. Always seek truth, no matter where it takes you." These were the tenets of our belief system.

As I grew into adulthood, I became increasingly thankful that I was raised with such a sane worldview. I felt bad for the Christians who seemed timid about learning, particularly when it came to the natural sciences, for fear of what they might find. I basked in the freedom of being able to think for myself on all matters. I especially pitied the Christians when it came to "sin." We atheists didn't live under oppressive, antiquated rules about right and wrong that prevented us from enjoying life; we were free to be good people for the pure reason of wanting to do good, not because some man in the sky told us what to do or because we feared eternal punishment.

I was so delighted with this freedom that I made a conscious effort to live a truly post-Christian life. For too long our society, even we atheists, had unconsciously borrowed from the archaic Judeo-Christian morals of our forebears. I began to make an effort to base my worldview and morality on purely atheistic principles. But this quickly led me to some surprising places.

Applying David Hume's famous epithet, author John C. Wright quipped of atheistic morality, "You cannot deduce an 'ought' from an 'is.'"[1] That is exactly the problem I faced as I attempted to be a "good person" from a completely secular perspective. My parents were deeply moral people who had raised me to be compassionate toward others and always observe the Golden Rule. Yet when I persisted in asking why, as I was taught to do, I could find no reason to place that set of values over other, more ruthless worldviews. Sure, humans may have evolved to have more cohesive communities or to be more peaceful when treating others well; on the other hand, each individual's likelihood of survival is increased when he dominates—or eradicates— other human beings. So is it better to be compassionate or discard others for your own well-being? The answer, I realized, could never be anything more than a matter of opinion.

I thought that I'd found true happiness but, somewhere in the back of my mind, I was aware that I had no peace, only surface-level feelings that were propped up on the quaking pillars of good health and good money.

Over and over again I found that my gut reactions about what was right and wrong were only barely defensible—if at all—in my belief system. I didn't like it, but I wasn't going to say that these conclusions weren't true just because they gave me a bad feeling.

I dealt with this conundrum in typical twenty-something fashion: I threw myself into work and partying. I graduated from college at the beginning of the dot-com boom and got a job at a hot high-tech start-up. I quickly began advancing in my career, my social life doing just as well. Between over-priced martinis in hip bars, first-class flights to interesting parts of the world, and increasingly impressive-sounding titles on my business cards, those looming questions that had once troubled me became pretty easy to ignore. I thought that I'd found true happiness.

But somewhere in the back of my mind, I was aware that I had no peace—only surface-level feelings that were propped up on the quaking pillars of good health and good money. I would continue to chase after fleeting happiness and ignore life's big questions until something made me stop and reevaluate everything: the birth of my first child.

I'd married a wonderful man named Joe whom I'd met at work. Sometimes it gave me chills to think that I almost didn't date him when I found out he believed in God. I'd always said that I'd only date atheists, but he was such a good catch that I made an exception. He'd grown up poor, and with sheer determination and intelligence, he had earned degrees from Yale, Columbia, and Stanford. The fact that he believed in God obviously hadn't impacted his ability to think clearly. And he didn't go to church or read the Bible or do any other "God stuff."

When our son was born a year into our marriage, I became acutely aware that I didn't have clarity on my own worldview. Looking down at the little dark-haired, eight-pound person and realizing that he'd be utterly dependent on me for shaping his outlook on life made me do some-thing I'd never done before: seek the truth *with humility*. I had always sought truth above all else but with a heaping dose of pride.

When I thought through big questions in quiet moments, without any pressure of wondering what people would think of me, I began to have doubts about atheism. I had to admit that you couldn't prove the supernatural either way; it was possible that something might exist outside the material world. I still saw zero evidence of gods or angels or anything like that, but I decided that I wouldn't pass on a purely atheistic worldview to my son.

I even tried saying a quick prayer—the first one I'd ever said in my life—just to see if anything would happen. I was surprisingly disappointed that my prayer was met with silence, and I assumed that meant that God didn't exist. But looking back I believe that that one half-hearted prayer opened the doors for the radically different route my life was about to take.

A few months later I stumbled across a book called *The Case for Christ*,[2] in which the author, a former atheist, laid out the case—based on reason, not quoting Bible verses—that Jesus was who he said he was. He also pointed out that Jesus made a shocking claim that no founder of any other major religion has ever made: that he was God himself. It struck me that that was a pretty bold claim, one that would doom a religion to collapse as soon as the guy was exposed as a fraud, unless there was something to it.

Though I didn't think that any of this would pan out upon further examination, I was curious about how Christianity survived with a founder who made such an outrageous claim. I began taking a closer look at this religion that I'd spent most of my life ridiculing. I discovered books by Christian converts like Augustine of Hippo, C.S. Lewis, and G.K. Chesterton. Their writings fascinated me because their thought processes were so lucid and their points so reasonable.

I became interested enough in Christianity to buy a Bible, the first I'd ever owned. (I was so embarrassed that I loudly told the cashier at the bookstore that it was a gift for a religious friend.) I said a little "God, if you exist, please help me" prayer and cracked open my new Bible with an air of electric anticipation. I was quickly disappointed. I couldn't make heads or tails of it.

After the Adam and Eve part, the story started to get really dense, and I had no idea what was going on. I didn't know what was supposed to be taken literally and what wasn't. I read aloud a passage from the book of Numbers about offering an unblemished sheep at the north side of an altar and sprinkling its blood around the other sides, and I guffawed to Joe, "Is this something I'm supposed to be doing?"

I was surprised that Jesus didn't come into the picture until much later in the book, and even then I wasn't sure what was going on. I expected the Bible to end with clear instructions about what to do next, like, "If you're convinced, just say a prayer and accept Jesus, and start going to church." But the last section was about some fantastical visions that I couldn't decipher. I felt lost and confused and wondered how anyone could ever convert to this religion without endless free time to pore over the Bible, let alone decent reading comprehension skills.

I tried looking for a church so that I could find people who could answer my questions, but this only confused me further. An Internet search showed hundreds of churches in my area, everything from Pentecostal to Anglican to Church of Christ to Baptist to Jehovah's Witnesses, and I had no idea where to go. They all claimed to be based on the Bible, but they all taught different things. Online searches for Christian websites showed that there seemed to be as many opinions about what Christianity taught as there were people. And everyone claimed that his or her opinions were based on the Bible.

I had to admit that this religion thing wasn't checking out. There didn't seem to be any consensus about what Christian doctrine was. And it didn't make sense that someone would have to be intelligent and educated enough to be a Bible scholar to figure out where to go to church on Sunday. This type of elitist, chaotic system didn't seem like something God would design, if he did exist.

Just when I was about to give up, an acquaintance proposed something shocking: that I should look into Catholicism. He explained the Catholic belief that Jesus founded a Church before he returned to heaven, and that it's recognizable today by the fact that all its leaders can be traced back as successors of the original guys who hung out with Jesus. The Catholics also claimed that God still, to this day, protects the Church from erring on matters of doctrine. In other words, you don't have to be a Bible scholar to know what this religion teaches, and you don't need to be at the mercy of other human beings who know the Bible better than you do. God took care of that by giving us a Church, which he guides.

I had always seen Catholicism as organized religion in its worst form, the Church of the Crusades and the Inquisition, oppressing people with guilt and antiquated rules. I was willing to take a second look, but how would I know if the Catholic hierarchy wasn't just creating a story in order to wield control over its followers? How would I know if this religion was guided by God and not just created by clever people?

After a lot of thought, I identified what I was looking for: the fingerprints of God. I'd need to see this faith produce something that humans could not do alone.

Joe was wary of this new turn of events. Having been raised Baptist, he had some strong anti-Catholic views of his own. Nevertheless, I needed to find out if there was anything to Catholicism before I gave up on Christianity altogether.

As my bedside table overflowed with books by Catholic authors like Pope Benedict XVI, Scott Hahn, Mark Shea, and Thomas Howard, I began to find something I'd never imagined I'd encounter in religious circles: people who questioned assumptions. These authors seemed to be willing to ask any tough question on any subject, from the sciences to theology and morality. If fact, it seemed that Catholic scholars were the most willing of any group of people I'd ever encountered—even atheists—to question assumptions.

When I read the *Catechism of the Catholic Church*, I was shocked at what I found. In it was an imminently reasonable, seamless moral code—one that resonated with what I believed in my heart to be good and true. Some of the teachings were the exact opposite of what I'd always believed, but I had to admit that the Church's defense of its positions was rational and intellectually consistent. The more I studied the hows and whys behind its doctrines, the more I felt as if I'd stumbled upon a road map to enlightenment and freedom.

Joe eventually became so intrigued by what I was finding that he began doing his own research. As our stacks of books about Catholicism multiplied, we were both shocked to find that we agreed with the Church on even its most controversial claims, such as its stance against abortion and contraception. Given the immense wisdom we found, oddly resonating on a deep level while being utterly counterintuitive, we began to seriously consider converting.

But that was all before the medical diagnosis. It had all seemed so simple when it was safely confined to the pages of a book. Now that following Catholic teaching would involve real consequences and real sacrifice, I wasn't so giddy.

The doctors were saying I had to use contraception to prevent future pregnancies, especially while on the postpartum medication to treat the clot. Though the Church does not teach that it's wrong to avoid pregnancy, it does emphasize the gravity of intentionally severing the marital act from its life-giving potential. I had a wealth of Catholic resources at my disposal for learning natural, non-contraceptive methods for avoiding pregnancy, but none offered the ease and security that I perceived I would have with contraception.

I talked about it with Joe, and I thought and even prayed about the situation as the day of my second doctor's appointment drew near. What I realized was that the truth of Catholic teaching on all matters, even contraception, was never really in question for me. I was tempted to walk away from it because it was hard and I was scared, not because I didn't think it was true.

I realized something else as well: When I thought through the option of not becoming Catholic, it almost caused me physical pain. I felt that to walk away from what I'd found in the Church would be to lose part of myself. This institution knew me better than I knew myself, and its teachings were a prescription for a rich life, not the set of confining rules I'd always imagined them to be.

I admonished myself to balance my thoughts by remembering all the sinful things Catholics have done throughout history. I thought of the wayward priests, immoral popes, religious oppressors, and every type of hypocrite that could be found in the church in the past and even today. But then it occurred to me: *These people* didn't screw up the Church. This institution, comprised of human beings no less prone to sin than anyone else, had survived for more than two thousand years, while empire after empire fell away around it. The Church has never reversed its teachings and has managed to produce a seamless worldview, profound moral code, and unfathomably deep body of wisdom on the human experience. Impossible. It really was, I realized, not something we fallible humans could do.

And that's when I knew that I had found the fingerprints of God.

Joe and I signed up for the Rite of Christian Initiation for Adults, the process for becoming Catholic, and I prepared to tell my doctor that I would not be willing to follow the standard treatment that involved contraception. It would be my first proclamation of faith after a life of atheism.

When the next appointment rolled around, I sat in the black leather patient's chair, my hands shaking a little. When the doctor sat down in his chair, I took a deep breath and began. "We're going to need to discuss an alternate treatment because…". After some hesitation I finally proclaimed, "Because…I, uhh, might be like, maybe, thinking about converting to Catholicism or something." It wasn't exactly from *The Lives of the Saints;* nevertheless it marked one of the biggest turning points of my life.

In the months that followed, the way was smoothed for me to stick to my newfound principles while still looking out for my health. Though my doctors remained baffled by my choices, they worked to get me on the shortest possible treatment plan with the drug that was incompatible with pregnancy. They also came up with specially tailored treatment plans to see me through future pregnancies.

Joe and I both entered the Catholic Church at Easter Vigil of the next year, shortly before our *third* child was born.

Many people asked if I was surprised to end up Catholic after a life of atheism. The surprise was not as much that I became Catholic as that the Catholic Church was not what I'd perceived it to be. My parents had taught me to keep searching for truth until I found it, and that's exactly what I did.

CHAPTER THREE

How the Raving Atheist Became the Raving Theist

www.ravingatheist.com

In December of 2008 a popular blogger known as "The Raving Atheist" announced his conversion to Christianity and changed the site's masthead to "The Raving Theist," dedicating it "to Jesus Christ, now and forever." The unbelievers in his readership reacted with a combination of vitriol and, for lack of a better word, unbelief. The Raving Atheist had frequently denounced such conversion stories as hoaxes and believed it could never happen to him, until he experienced for himself what he now knows was God's grace. Nor did his readers have the benefit of the account he is about to give.

I grew up in a largely secular area of Long Island. My mother was the daughter of a Protestant minister, and my father was an agnostic whose family was once active in Communist circles. Although I attended my mother's church every week until sixth grade, it was more for cultural and social reasons than spiritual ones.

I didn't have a relationship with God; that wasn't even something we talked about. But I remember once, when I was seven or eight years old, my mother fainted, and my first reaction was to run upstairs and pray about it, to ask God for help.

During my last year of high school, I began taking a greater interest in religion. I'd become close friends with a Reform Jewish kid who had a brilliant scientific mind and who openly mocked religion. That year I read Bertrand Russell's essay "Why I Am Not a Christian." I was captivated by the irreverent humor and whimsical tone. His reasoning made perfect sense to me, and by the time I entered college, I considered myself an atheist as well. (My conviction was such that I saw fit to dramatically—and quite irrelevantly—proclaim that fact in the opening sentence of a cover letter seeking a PBS internship.)

In the summer after my freshman year of college, I hopped a bus to California, excited by the prospect of adventures out West. My enthusiasm quickly waned after a couple of weeks on skid row and a failed stint as a door-to-door encyclopedia salesman. I settled into a clerical job and found less seedy lodgings, then spent much of my free time holed up in the Los Angeles library, reading about cults and deprogramming. In addition to having a devout Scientologist landlady, I'd begun noticing the Moonies all over L.A.

One afternoon I just happened to loiter near a corner where the Moonies were proselytizing. They invited me into their group, and I hung out with them for a weekend retreat in the San Bernardino Mountains. When they tried to convince me to send for all my worldly belongings, my suspicions were confirmed. I packed my bags and headed back to college, determined to write about my experiences and my conviction that all religions were cults.

The piece I wrote helped formulate most of my thoughts about religion. Eventually it was published in the college newspaper, although the editors cut a section that attempted to draw unflattering parallels between the Moonies and the Catholic Church.

After college I had little time to think about religion or atheism. I was too busy going to law school and having a life. My career as a lawyer flourished, and eventually I began teaching law as well.

In the late nineties I attended a series of continuing education courses in philosophy. The professor, a philosopher who edited and wrote the introduction to Bertrand Russell's collection of essays, was very sarcastic. He hated religion and religious people. I got to know him and soon was engaging in debate with other lawyers about atheism. My focus on atheism as a lifestyle led a friend to suggest that I begin a blog.

So in late 2001 I began cowriting a political blog with a college acquaintance, my posts focusing frequently on religion. Soon I started my own blog attacking religious people as demented, deluded "Godidiots." I wrote scathing essays explaining how the "culture of belief" was destroying America. I would track down faith-based blogs, ridicule their motives as suspect, and pronounce them guilty of insanity—despite the fact that these people lived simple, good lives.

True atheism, I believed, was not about "live and let live." It was a cause that needed an evangelist as much as any faith. In an effort to provide a set of atheistic principles for such a ministry, the "basic assumptions" of my blog declared that all definitions of God either were self-contradictory, incoherent, and meaningless or could be refuted by empirical, scientific evidence.

Despite my bold posturing, I felt ill-versed in scientific matters, and I recognized that my "logical disproofs" could only go so far. In fact, in an early essay I conceded that it was technically possible for a rational person to have a belief in God. To my mind, however, it was still only possible in the sense that one might be sharing the room with a purple hippopotamus that evaded detection by darting away the moment one tried to turn around and see it. In other words, there was no evidence for it. So while it was a possibility, it wasn't worth much consideration.

At the very instant that the wafer touched my lips, an angry, mocking voice from behind hissed, "So much for the atheist."

In late 2002 I attended a blogger party where I sat next to a Catholic blogger named Benjamin. At one point the conversation turned to abortion, and I asked Benjamin's opinion of the practice. The calm, confident reply was: "It's murder." I was stunned. Here was a kind, affable, and cogently reasonable human being who nonetheless believed that abortion was murder. To the limited extent I had previously considered the issue, I believed abortion to be completely acceptable, the mere disposal of a lump of cells, perhaps akin to clipping fingernails.

This unsettling exchange spurred me to further investigate the issue on Benjamin's blog. I noticed that pro-choice Christians did not employ scientific or rational arguments but relied on a confused set of "spiritual" platitudes. More significantly, the overwhelmingly pro-choice atheistic blogosphere also fell short in its analysis of abortion. The supposedly "reality-based" community either dismissed abortion as a "religious issue" or paradoxically claimed that pro-life principles were contrary to religious doctrine. Having formerly equated atheism with reason, I was slowly growing uncertain of the value of godlessness in the search for truth.

I nevertheless continued my atheistic ravings full force. In early 2003 I engaged in a particularly venomous exchange with an online Catholic scholar over Thomas Aquinas's "first cause" argument. In a later, conciliatory gesture, I linked to a post-abortion healing blog favored by my religious adversary—an act that brought me into contact with a group of pro-life advocates whose selfless dedication to their cause moved me deeply. I was inspired by their gentle and reasonable writings, particularly the story of a woman named Ashli, who wrote with painful honesty about how her late-term abortion had affected her. She now channeled her suffering into efforts to help women in similar situations and save them from the fallout of abortion.

I began communicating with Ashli, and eventually she asked for my assistance in some of her pro-life work. When she gave birth to a healthy baby girl on Mother's Day 2004, I decided to use the occasion to announce that the Raving Atheist would become, in part, a pro-life blog. This decision stirred an angry mutiny among my readers. But I had become convinced that the secular world had it wrong on the very foundational issue of life.

With Ashli's encouragement I began volunteering at a crisis pregnancy center. Suddenly I was surrounded by life. Here were people who were kind and loving and who lived out their faith in a very tangible way. The pictures on the walls of the center confirmed this. Smiling babies were everywhere. The tangible expression of pro-life work was life itself. It was becoming clear to me that people who lived out their Christian faith were happier and better people as a result.

Despite this evidence I maintained a lingering intellectual attachment to atheism. In late 2004 I organized a blog interview with the bestselling atheist author Sam Harris (*The End of Faith*). Assisting in the questioning was filmmaker Brian Flemming. This association led both me and Harris to appear the next year in Flemming's anti-Christian documentary, *The God Who Wasn't There*.

I attended the documentary's New York premiere. At the end of a subsequent summertime showing in the city, however, I found my atheistic enthusiasm waning. The appearance of my pseudonym in the credits inspired less pride than I had expected. As the lights turned on, I felt alienated from the audience and its contemptuous, antireligious laughter.

I briefly considered joining a small group that had formed to discuss the film over dinner. In fact I followed them for several blocks while debating whether to invite myself. But halfway across a darkened midtown street, I walked away.

That fall I began a friendship with a Catholic blogger, Dawn. I frequently guest posted on her site about pro-life issues. I also continued working on certain "hard cases" with Ashli. Near Thanksgiving of 2005, Ashli opened her heart (and home) to a young woman coping with a particularly difficult and tumultuous pregnancy. Dawn, other bloggers, and I came together on this woman's behalf.

In June 2006 I saw the woman's sonogram ripen into a baby. In honor of Ashli's efforts, I vowed that the birth of the child would spell the death of atheism on my blog. Late that month I announced that I would no longer mock God on my site.

Although still a doubter, my subsequent posts entertained the possibility of God. I asked Dawn if I could join her at church, and at her suggestion I began daily prayer. I still didn't believe in God, but I wanted to change. I wanted the deep, abiding joy I'd observed in my pro-life Christian friends.

Because of Dawn's great kindness to me, in the summer of 2006 my wife and I began attending church with her. On July 23 we went together to the Church of Our Saviour on Park Avenue and 38th Street. I walked up for Communion (though I learned later that I shouldn't have). At the very instant that the wafer touched my lips, an angry, mocking voice from behind hissed, "So much for the atheist."

I returned to the pew but said nothing. I tried to tell myself that I had misheard what was said, although the voice was so articulate that there was really no doubt in my mind. Colin, a friend of Dawn, had been in line several people behind me. He sat down next to me and asked if I had heard the same thing he had. He had looked at the speaker (I had not), a disheveled and possibly schizophrenic man. Colin did not realize that the timing of the utterance coincided with my taking Communion.

Dawn, also behind me in the Communion line, was late in returning to the pew. Having heard the same thing, she had scooted off to a row of candles to say a prayer for me. Very matter-of-factly she hypothesized that Satan had been stirred. He was enraged at the prospect of losing one of his most "faithful" advocates.

Ninety-five percent of me was blowing the incident off as coincidence. My main concern was that I would never hear the end of it or, worse yet, that Dawn would post about it without my permission. My atheistic instincts compelled me to categorize the event as the sort of worthless spiritual personal experience that nonbelievers immediately recognize as a sign of credulity, mental illness, or simple lying. I was ashamed to even pretend to take it seriously.

Two witnesses though. It did make enough of an impression on me that I memorialized it as my "Quote of the Day" that evening. And freed from the compulsion to launch a blog-attack on God, I was eventually able to view the incident as a rational person should: if not conclusive proof, at least evidence pointing distinctly in one direction.

I applied this approach to my consideration of theology in general. In time I found it impossible to believe that the universe was created out of nothing. There was order, direction, and love. Those things all pointed to some larger, unfathomable consciousness. I realized I could not believe that human hearts and minds came into being randomly.

My eyes were also opened to the core truth of Christianity. Whereas I had formerly concurred with Nietzsche's appraisal of the faith as a "slave's philosophy," a cruel celebration of senseless suffering, I saw that his experiences had brought even him to appreciate the nobility of sacrifices made for the sake of life.

CHAPTER FOUR

———

"The LORD Is God! The LORD Is God!" (1 Kings 18:39)
Mattie Berhang

Mattie Berhang was raised in New York City. She trained in the arts and sciences, traveled widely, and made her living as a sculptor until her conversion. Presently she lives on a mountain outside Ellenville, New York.

In 1949, when I was six years old, my father took me to see the Metropolitan Museum's splendiferous retrospective of Vincent van Gogh's work. In his awe at what he saw, my father remarked in a soft, stunned voice, "Van Gogh is immortal."

"What does *immortal* mean?" I asked.

"It means that you will never die, that you will live forever."

I embraced that thought literally, as a child would. It went right into my heart, to remain there "for always." To live forever became the quest of my soul.

My parents were Jews but did not practice. Mom prayed every day but did not respect organized religion. Pop, much influenced by Freud, was an atheist until his late seventies, when he moved toward agnosticism. I never knew what Mom thought about the afterlife, but Pop stated emphatically and often, "When you're dead, you're *dead!*" Against this background I kept the secret of my heart: "I want to live forever."

We lived in an apartment on East 96th Street in Manhattan. Both my parents worked, and I could read, so my big after-school adventure was to cross Lexington Avenue (very carefully) and go to the "big people's library." The library had a large picture window that looked across 96th Street to the Church of St. Francis de Sales. I would watch two lines of nuns—mysterious, silent presences in long black dresses with their faces framed in white—ascend the seemingly endless steps and enter the church for Holy Mass.

Once I asked my mother who they were, and she said, "They are Catholic nuns."

"What are nuns?"

"It's a Catholic thing," she said. "You don't need to know." But I kept their mystery in my heart.

About that time I asked my father, "Daddy, who is God?"

He responded with a certain assurance, "God is somebody we made up because we needed him."

"Who is Jesus?"

"Jesus was our rabbi. Some people thought he was God."

The teachers at my school, P.S. 59, were old; Mom called them "retreads" because they came back from retirement to teach the "old method" in contrast to the "progressive method." Most of them were Catholic. Miss Gillespie was my favorite, a gentle, sweet, caring lady. I still have the picture I took of her with my Baby Brownie camera.

One day Miss Gillespie and some of the children came in with black marks on their foreheads. "What's that?" I whispered to my friend Joanie.

"It's a special thing we get at church for Lent." Joanie couldn't say what Lent was, and I wouldn't be so forward as to ask a teacher something personal like that. "Another Catholic mystery," I pondered.

Fast-forward to graduation from the Bronx High School of Science, whither I'd gone to please my parents. I was seventeen years old and would start at Temple University's Tyler School of Art in the fall. In those days one did not leave home or take a job without parental permission before age eighteen. So I hired out as a mother's helper to a family with two young girls. They offered a summer on Nantucket, which sounded like a real adventure. So paint box in hand, off I went.

As I saw myself an artist and carried Van Gogh's self-portrait with me everywhere, I affected dirty, paint-spattered clothes; stringy, oily hair; sandals on dirty feet; and a "beat" attitude: "I am gifted. I am sensitive. I am superior to mortal flesh." ("And ye shall be as gods," Genesis 3:5, *KJV.*) The father of the two girls thought me a bad influence and told me to get out. He gave me no money for either wages or transport.

I had no money of my own, so I couldn't get off the island. The local police were very compassionate, helping me get my things and mentioning to my former employer that I was a minor and wages needed to be paid. He was obdurate, so the police put me up in the jail until I could get my sea legs. Following their advice, I filed a small claims suit for my wages and fare. While waiting for the court appearance, I stayed where I could and took on odd jobs.

One day I decided to go swimming on Surfside Beach, the Nantucket shore that faces the roughest seas. I was alone, a storm was brewing, and the waves were huge, but with the presumption of my youth and strength, I went out anyway. There was a fierce undertow, and before I realized it, I was out too far to swim back.

God is either God of everything or God of nothing.

Wave upon wave hit me. I went under, came up, gasped, and went under again. I was drowning. They say there are no atheists in foxholes. I appealed to God and lost consciousness.

The next thing I knew, I was lying on Surfside with water streaming out of my nose and mouth, and a guy named Frank was giving me CPR. He had been walking his dog and had seen my hand above the water. By God's grace, he was a lifeguard at another beach.

The Tyler School of Art came and went. The pursuit of immortality continued.

In October 1965, now twenty-one, I was hitchhiking through England. In Reading a guy stopped for me, and I told him my destination. After some time it came to me: "He's driving in the wrong direction." I voiced my doubts; no comment. I asked him to let me off; he stepped on the gas. We were in the middle of nowhere. I thought, "I'm done. This guy's gonna kill me."

Hugging my pack in front of me to cushion my fall, I opened the door and jumped. The ditch I landed in was deep but dry. Scrambling up the bank onto the roadway, I saw the car turning around and heading straight for me. "God, help me! Please! Now!"

I saw another car coming from the opposite direction. Frantic with fright, I practically threw myself in front of it. The good people listened to my plea, took me to the local police and then to their farm, where I stayed for a few days. The grandmother who lived there remarked, "God has preserved you." She gave me a little Bible, which I still have.

I was in Manila for Holy Week in 1968 and saw people inching toward the cathedral on torn and bleeding knees. Some carried small crosses or crucifixes; others prayed the rosary as they crawled. The faith in the air was palpable. My heart was pierced by a lance of desire: "I want that. I want that. O mystery of the Catholic faith!"

Weeks later, still in Manila, I was sitting with my English beau in the balcony of the Aloha Movie Theater watching *Love With a Proper Stranger.* Suddenly the balcony started to move. People screamed and ran for the stairwells.

"Let's go!" I cried. "Let's get out of here!"

"Sit down and watch the movie."

"We've seen it before! We know the end!"

"It's an earthquake. You can't get out. They'll trample you to death. Sit down and watch the movie. If I'm going to die, I'm going to die with dignity."

I sat down. The swinging stopped, and the screaming turned to wailing. We walked out, stepping around the bodies of those who had been trampled. The columns that had supported the ceiling of the theater were broken in half. If they had shifted just a little farther, that would have been the end of us.

As the aftershocks continued, I considered God's mercy, perhaps for the first time. When solid ground is no longer something you can count on, you wonder, "What indeed can I count on?"

In 1970 I returned to New York, seeking placement for my artwork, thrills, and romance. As part of my artist image, I believed it right and even necessary to do outlandish things—art as a cloak for vice. To that end I became passionately involved with a dissolute, abusive, and thoroughly nasty man.

One day, after a particularly wild time, I looked in the mirror and thought, "If this continues I will be dead." By now I believed that God existed, and for the first time I begged him to change my life, knowing I could not.

Soon after my prayer I met a painter named Al at the Laundromat. He invited me to a party, where I drank a lot and became hysterical. I told Al about the dangerous situation I was in and how I was afraid to go home. Good soul that he was, he took me to my house, faced down my tormentor, and stayed with me until we were both convinced that I was out of danger.

It was through Al that I met Sean. Sean was that *rara avis*, a serious Catholic and a serious artist. As we had equally abrasive personalities, we hit it off really well. He looked at my work and said, "I refuse to even talk about art with you until you go to the Studio School." I respected Sean, so I did just that.

Our teacher was the sculptor George Spaventa. He was the artist's artist. He stayed in his studio, worked day and night, taught to eat, and was absolutely focused on the life of works of art, which he summed up in the phrase "It is." I worked with him for three years.

One night I was cooking spaghetti when I received a phone call. George had been found dead in his bathtub. The shock was unreal. The sun had gone out. This man, the artist-saint, had *died*. So much for immortality.

Sean and Al and I went to the funeral at St. Lucy in the Bronx. All I could think was, "Art is *not* the guarantor of immortality. What am I going to do now?"

Sean said, "I think it's time you started reading the Bible." I'd tried on and off for years to read the King James Version, but he said, "Get a Bible you can *read*. Try the Jerusalem Bible."

The Jerusalem Bible was thrilling to me. It is heavily footnoted and cross-referenced, readable as well as scholarly. I read it straight through, looking up every reference and cross-reference. When I had questions I called Sean. My mind often reeled with our conversations, scrolling them over and over.

Then Sean's house burned down. He escaped with his life, his son, and the clothes he had on. He sent his son to live with his estranged wife and called me. "Of course, come here," I said.

Sean's life was destroyed. His paintings, books, clothing, shoes, legal papers, checkbooks, everything was gone. He made lists to keep himself together, and every fourth item was "Pray." He went to Mass every day. I was in awe. Sean got himself together and moved out. But the trail was blazed.

I began to pray—not just occasionally but all the time, every day. I did not know how to pray really, so I asked God to teach me. I read the Psalms over and over. My personal prayer often started with the bottom of Psalm 86:

> Teach me thy way, O LORD;
>> I will walk in thy truth:
>> unite my heart to fear thy name.
> I will praise thee, O Lord my God, with all my heart:
>> and I will glorify thy name for evermore.
> For great is thy mercy toward me:
>> and thou hast delivered my soul from the lowest
>> hell. (Psalm 86:11–13, *KJV*)

The success of my work overrode the desire of my heart for immortality. Reputation, fame, and money for a little while silenced the voice that had wailed at George's funeral, "What am I going to do now?"

Sean kept after me. "Are you starting to believe your own press? Keep searching for Truth."

One day I came to and realized, "My life is about making baubles for the rich." An emptiness chilled my heart.

In the street a guy was broadsiding Jews for Jesus. I'd concluded from Scripture that Jesus is the Messiah. In my mind the majority of Jews had missed the boat. But Jews for Jesus? Maybe they won the lottery.

I decided to go to a meeting. They were lovely people. I thought I was home. The warm fuzzies were short-lived, however. As I listened to the preaching week after week, it seemed to me that it was heavy on sin but light on forgiveness. As I'd lived a sinful life, I desperately wanted God's forgiveness. I called Sean.

"It's a Baptist theology," he said. "Talk to a priest."

I'd gone a few times to a nearby church, so I went back there and, in great excitement, slid into the last pew just before the bell rang for the entrance of the priest. After Mass I walked up to him and said, "Father, I think I'd like to take instruction."

He looked at me as if I were covered with roaches and said, "I can't help you. I have too much to do."

I felt so bad. I went down the steps holding the handrail, unable to see for the tears. My heart was torn open. At home I had a couple of shots, read some Scripture, and prayed for God's help, love, and mercy.

I continued to pray by myself, study Holy Scripture, make sculpture, and go to Jews for Jesus gatherings. Sean gave me some tapes of Br. David Steindl-Rast preaching on prayer and on the interpretation of sacred Scripture, which I played over and over, trying to digest every morsel that was offered.

The sculpture began to reflect my spiritual journey. My 1982 show at OK Harris Gallery included a piece called "*Hineni*," which is Hebrew for "Here I Am," the traditional Jewish prophet's answer to God's call, and "Tabernacle," which alluded to Moses' tabernacle.

One day at that exhibition, a tiny, radiant woman entered the gallery and stayed for a long time, examining the pieces with interest. Something about her drew me. "Excuse me," I said, "but I have to meet you. Who are you?"

"I'm Arden Scott," she replied. We talked a little about the work and decided to go for a drink. Over our beers we discussed sculpture, which was a common bond, her family, and her politics and religion.

Arden was a Dorothy Day Catholic. Her "house of hospitality" was open to anyone, human or animal, who needed help. She cared for her own four children, her husband, and literally anyone who came along—the sick, the disillusioned, the bitter, the penniless, the grimy, the addicted, the homeless, the unwanted. There wasn't a lot of money, but there were always peanut butter sandwiches, sleeping bags, sympathetic ears, and a shoulder to cry on. She impressed me very much.

Arden spoke to me a great deal abut Christ—in words, in her selfless and constant giving, and in her great and obvious joy in life, children, animals, and art. Like Sean, she gave me books and prayers and taught me Catholic traditions you would never get in a formal class.

At Sean's yearly Epiphany party, I met Fr. David, a pleasant, quiet fellow with an Irish surname. He seemed more approachable than the first priest, so I made an appointment to see him at his church. The day of our interview, I prayed, "Teach me thy way, O Lord," but sat on my excitement, approaching the meeting warily.

Father welcomed me into his study. I told him I might want to receive instruction but had a question before making such a deep commitment.

Fr. David pursed his lips. "A question before we even start?"

"Yes, Father. Do you believe in random and chance?"

"Well, of course, I do. Much of what happens is one or the other."

"Thank you, Father. I'm sorry I troubled you." I extended my hand. He shook it, and I left.

I lost my shirt on my 1985 show. To do something wonderful and life-affirming, I took the last of what was in the bank and went to Italy. It was glorious. I returned dead broke and went to Ellenville, New York, to bang nails into what I hoped would be my retirement home. When it was time to return to the art world and New York, I found myself depressed. An inspiration came: "No one has put a gun to your head. Don't go back."

The 1990 show, with the Carlo Lamagna Gallery, was all made in Ellenville. Commissions kept me alive. The pieces more and more reflected the call of the Lord. One was "In the Desert"; another, "Piece without Words," was inspired by T.S. Eliot's "Ash Wednesday." I also worked with an organic farmer, Ralph Swenson, who taught me to love the mystery of growth and the smell of soil.

Eventually I needed a "real" job. I took one as a bellhop at the local Homowack Lodge. The great thing about this job was that it was all sweat. All I had to remember was a three-digit room number or the make and color of a car. Lots of room for God—and other things.

Among the passing parade was a wild kind of guy who raised dogs and expressed an interest in me. As I raised dogs too, we had a meeting ground. The lights went on and off with us, two difficult people. After a while it depressed me. I called Sean.

He said, "Mattie, I'm tired of having this conversation with you. There's a priest named Fr. Richard Neilson at the Church of Our Saviour on 38th Street and Park Avenue. I want you to go and see him."

The next day I called. Father could see me the following week. Anticipation. Dread. Would I strike out again? Would I get lucky?

Fr. Neilson was small and slight, with a pronounced Scottish accent. "Well, my dear, so you think you want to take instruction?"

"Yes, Father, but I want to ask you something first."

"Go ahead."

"Father, do you believe in random or chance?"

He replied, "No, my dear, certainly not! God is either God of everything or God of nothing."

Joy, relief, and gratitude flooded my heart. I'd found my teacher! Before I left he blessed me in the name of Almighty God, with the tenderness of a mother comforting a wounded child. "I have the 7 AM Mass on Thursday," he said gently. "I'll offer it for you."

Fr. Neilson was the soul of patience. Apologetics was his strong suit. He answered my endless questions with precision, care, and compassion. He assured me that no matter how much time he spent teaching me, if I concluded that God was not calling me to enter the church, I should not feel obligated to him. I prized this consideration. It removed anxiety and pressure and gave me freedom to learn, to doubt, to ask, and to let the struggle between belief and unbelief run its course.

Because of the stubbornness of my doubts, my intellectual pride, the depths of my ignorance, and Father's conscientious thoroughness, the battle raged for a year and a half. Finally Father said, "My dear, I believe you are ready."

Ebullient and petrified, I called Sean to ask him to be my godfather.

"Yeah, sure, Mattie. Where's the party?" Then he warned me, "Look, if you're coming into the church, just remember, you have to love her—warts and all."

Arden was full of joy at hearing my news and delighted to serve as godmother. Her enthusiasm buoyed me up and dispelled my anxiety.

In the fullness of time, we gathered in the sanctuary of Our Saviour. I felt Arden's hand on my shoulder and Sean's gently gathering my long hair as I bowed my head over the water. Then Father intoned, "I baptize you in the name of the Father [splash], and of the Son [splash], and of the Holy Spirit [splash]." He dipped his thumb in sacred chrism and traced a cross on my forehead, saying, "Be sealed with the Gift of the Holy Spirit." Then I received the Body and Blood of the Lord for the first time. "With joy you will draw water at the fountain of salvation" (Isaiah 12:3, *NAB*). It was July 26, 1993.

In 1995, when my last commission was finished, I returned the certificate of authority for my business to New York State, severing my bonds with the art world. "No one can serve two masters" (Matthew 6:24, *NAB*).

Through the ups and downs of the last eighteen years, including offended family and friends and a considerable reduction in worldly wealth, I have never regretted my conversion. Life has never been so full or so rich, and I have gained the communion of saints, the forgiveness of sins, the resurrection of the body, and *life everlasting*. Amen.

Blessed be God! Alleluia!

CHAPTER FIVE

A Counterculture That Does Not Disappoint
Paul Vitz

Paul Vitz studied psychology at the University of Michigan; he then completed a PH.D. at Stanford University. After teaching and practicing psychology at New York University for over three decades, he retired from NYU and now teaches at the Institute for the Psychological Sciences. He lives in New York with his wife, Timmie, with whom he has six grown children.

The moments in life that lead you to convert might not seem obvious to some. I remember a former friend (and atheist) commenting happily over dinner in the early seventies, "Oh, isn't it wonderful to live in an age of decadence?" I was not amused by his attitude—and I credit it for moving me toward my eventual conversion! I imagine he would be surprised that his words had that effect. But those who know me better would not be.

I was born in Toledo, Ohio, in 1935 and raised in Minneapolis and Cincinnati. My parents had met at the library where they both worked. My mother was already in her mid-thirties, and I think she had assumed she'd never marry. She married my dad after his first wife (the mother of five children) died unexpectedly. So instead of the quiet life she'd imagined, my mother found herself with five young and teenaged stepchildren and, shortly thereafter, four sons of her own, of whom I was the oldest. It was a real shock to her system—especially as my dad was from a very German family, and my mother was of solid English farming stock.

My family attended a Presbyterian church in Cincinnati—though we went for mostly social rather than religious reasons. Neither of my parents was especially religious, nor did they speak to me much about religion. I attended some Sunday school and learned some Christian doctrine, but it had little impact on me. Christianity seemed nice but not very convincing or appealing.

Strangely, while my father was never a believer, he was very proud of the religious family he came from. He loved telling us that his own grandfather, a minister, had had nine children—all of whom had either become or married ministers!

In 1953 I left Cincinnati and started college at the University of Michigan. In high school I had been mostly interested in extracurriculars, but at Michigan I became a serious student. I soon settled on psychology as my major.

It became clear to me that the important psychologists, from Freud to Skinner, were atheists. Psychology (like most academic disciplines) operated on the assumption that religion was false—indeed rather backward and in the process of disappearing—as science and modern thought advanced toward their inevitable worldwide triumph. I quickly picked up this general attitude; it appealed to me at once. It allowed me to escape from my "provincial" past and to join my new profession without intellectual or moral liabilities from my nominally Christian upbringing.

In my sophomore year in college (appropriately enough), I decided that I was an atheist. It was no big change in my life, since I hadn't been much of a Christian to begin with. But my atheism also soon receded into the background, to be replaced by a general disinterest in religion.

Yet I had always had a deep sense of restlessness, an intense, unfocused searching. This ever-present longing, or *sehnsucht*, is one of my earliest memories. I imagine it's what St. Augustine was talking about when he referred to the restless heart we all have.[1] I put much of my restless energy into studying hard to become a professor of psychology. Careerism basically became the religion of my life. Yet some of the nagging restlessness remained. In fact, it would never really go away until my conversion.

In 1957 I graduated from the University of Michigan and began graduate studies at Stanford. There I found myself on the edge of what later became the "counterculture." Many of the people I worked and studied with were pioneers in the move to drugs and sexual liberation.

Richard Alpert was my first research advisor and a friend for a while. Not long afterward he left Stanford for Harvard and became famous—with Timothy Leary—for his LSD

> *All my life I had known good Christians: nice, solid, dependable people. But in the Catholic Church, I started meeting people who were not just "good"; they were **holy**.*

capers. At Stanford I lived near Perry Lane, where Alpert and Ken Kesey also lived. I visited them fairly often, drove Alpert's motorcycle (before getting my own), and so on.

I found the counterculture pretty exciting. Just like California itself, it was a new and fascinating world. I felt at ease in it, though it was never quite home.

After Stanford I had a couple of short-term teaching positions. In September 1965 I took a tenure-track position in the psychology department at New York University. A good bit of the hippie culture moved from California to the East Coast at around the same time I did. All around me I saw people trying to remake the world and new movements springing up with them. There was the Afro-centric movement, the feminist movement, then the gay movement: I was surrounded by what I'd call emergent radical tribalisms.

The old ways of understanding identity were slipping away, and new ways were taking their place. All these groups were antiestablishment in their focus, and they made me wonder about myself. What was my identity? What did I stand for? The nature of these movements made it clear that I wouldn't fit into them, but it wasn't clear how I *could* understand myself.

By the late sixties or early seventies, I wasn't sure what direction to go in. Adding to my confusion was a growing concern that many of the models and goals we were using in my field of experimental and cognitive psychology were deeply unethical. They seemed to be based on an idea of the human mind that seemed totally wrong to me. It was as if the purpose of science was to reduce the mind to a completely understandable thing—in a very deterministic way. I didn't really think this was even possible, but if it was, I did not want to be a part of it.

There was one bright spot: In the fall of 1968, I met Timmie Birge. She immediately caught my eye: She was very pretty, and she remembered my name right away. (It turned out a distant relative of mine had been a Latin teacher at her school.) We took walks in Washington Square Park, and unlike most people I met in New York (who weren't too familiar with nature), she even knew what a gingko tree was!

Something about Timmie and her Midwestern roots made her both familiar and admirable. From the very beginning she seemed "right." After we started dating, we discovered that we had almost rented apartments in the same building. We were married in August 1969. Timmie wasn't religious either. We made up our own marriage vows without any reference to God.

After my marriage many things converged to stir up the restlessness I had sensed since my childhood. I was growing less and less satisfied with the lifestyles and values that I saw my secular friends and colleagues espousing. In 1971 Timmie and I had our first child, Rebecca. The experience of fatherhood confronted me with a number of urgent questions. I had to give concrete answers to what truly mattered to me—what values and ideals I wanted for my daughter.

We were living in downtown Manhattan, in Greenwich Village, and the idea of raising a child in that weird place was a concern for me. I found myself with other anxieties: anxiety about money and how I could afford a family, anxiety about my career and how I could maintain an intense work schedule alongside the commitments of family life;

worry that my kids wouldn't have friends (who has friends in a city?). I laugh now, seeing the number of friends my children have. But at the time my fears were very real to me.

In the fall of 1972 I took my first sabbatical year. While I had many professional plans, the Holy Spirit seemed to have other ideas. Instead of dealing with my career, I found myself driven by a search for meaning: who I was and what I stood for. As I saw it, there were four basic options: leftist politics, Eastern religion, self-worship (focusing on career and so on), and traditional religion. I had tried, or seen others try, a, b, and c and could not accept them. The only option left was d, and for me that meant Christianity.

Fortunately, my wife was also experiencing an awakening of her religious interests, so together we visited a local Presbyterian church. We were uninspired, but a search for a church began in earnest. One day—I'm not quite sure how—we ended up at St. Thomas Episcopal Church in New York. I was moved and impressed by the liturgy and the preaching. I was also surprised and inspired during this period to discover how intellectually defensible Christianity was. I started reading works by C.S. Lewis and G.K. Chesterton and recognizing the power of Christian positions.

Much to our surprise, Timmie and I found ourselves most attracted to traditional Christianity—and especially to the Catholic Church. (Given my awareness of the hollowness of secular liberal thought and its values, seeing those values on display in a liberal Christian church was more than I could take.) Timmie and I started backing away from Protestantism and looking more and more toward Rome.

While traditional Christianity steadily increased its appeal, I also found it a real challenge to me on various fronts. I realized that I would need to rethink, in many ways, my whole approach to psychology. The idea of rethinking my career as it then existed was very difficult—and exacerbated by the fact that I didn't know a single other Christian psychologist! (All the "Christian" psychologists I knew had *lost* their faith!)

One of the things that really helped my slow but definitive professional transition was the publication of my first book, in 1977, *Psychology as Religion: The Cult of Self-Worship*. In it I critiqued humanistic psychology (the most popular psychology at the time). The enthusiastic response that this book received from many Christians showed me that I wasn't alone in my convictions and kept me intellectually engaged in my work (though I had no sympathetic colleagues at NYU, due to my conversion). Through the years the friendship of many Christians—often evangelical Protestants, usually far from New York—has had a major effect on me, helping me see my work from within a radically new community rather than something to be done alone and in isolation.

Another major factor in my—our—movement toward Catholicism was a number of really impressive people we met. All my life I had known good Christians: nice, solid, dependable people. But in the Catholic Church, I started meeting people who were not just "good"; they were *holy*. There were a number of priests Timmie and I met: Msgr. Eugene Kevane, Fr. James Halligan, and Fr. Benedict Groeschel (founder of the Franciscan Friars of the Renewal) especially come to mind. Their lives and personalities were marked by a sort of transcendence that was striking to me. I could see their prayerful closeness to God in the way they did everything.

Along with this strong attachment to the Lord, there was a lack of attachment to this world. I could sense the freedom that their holiness gave them. Lots of people try to be good; they try to be polite. There's nothing wrong with that, but it can demonstrate an attachment to the evaluation of the world: being nice so that other people respect and like you. These priests weren't good in that way; their goodness went beyond themselves. What I saw in them suggested that Catholicism was truly different from the other Christian churches I had been exposed to.

Several religious experiences also prepared the way for my conversion. They caught me by surprise and deepened my faith. The first few—they were like visions—happened over a ten-day period in September of 1977.

The first one revealed to me the existence, power, and majesty of God. I awakened early in the morning and saw myself looking up at an enormous person with a long robe; it was like standing at the bottom of a fifty-story building. As I touched the robe, it turned into a great curtain, which seemed to move off to the right, opening before me. I was overwhelmed by the space that I saw: It was infinite in all respects and seemed empty except for a glowing light and quiet but for an awesome low hum. I knew I was in the presence of God and was being shown his existence. After a few moments I saw a tiny dot from far away that started moving toward me. As it got closer, it moved faster as well, and I saw that it was Christ on the cross.

My other visions also helped me recognize the truth of what I had discovered in the church. One revealed to me the futility of trying to grasp a final or definitive theology through reason alone; another showed me the reality of sin, especially my own personal sin; the last one (in 1978) revealed the reality of the Risen Christ and my own personal relationship with him. Along with the Mass, prayer, reading, and Catholic friends, these visions solidified my commitment to the Catholic faith.

It was a great surprise that I became a Christian and then a Catholic. That it happened at all was a miracle, but that it also happened to my wife, Timmie, during the same time period was a double miracle! We have walked the road together. Over the decades, my life in the faith has been a rich, deepening, and ongoing challenge. Many people have helped along the way, especially Timmie and our six children. And of course, many wonderful priests and sisters have inspired me.

Who knows what lies ahead on this surprising road? While it is helpful sometimes to look back, the prize lies ahead, and I pray to be able to finish the race.

——

CHAPTER SIX

A Family United by the Spirit

Anonymous

I am now sixty-two years old. I became Catholic when I was thirty-four, after twelve years of marriage. My wife, Mary (not her real name), is a cradle Catholic, and she went to Mass every Sunday. She would tell you she was a bad Catholic when we met, but I believe I fell in love with her because of her faith.

My dad had been brought up Lutheran, and my mom was raised Episcopalian, but they didn't practice their faiths. We didn't go to church. My parents' attitude was that religion was something I could decide for myself when I became an adult. I remember going by a Catholic church in New Canaan, Connecticut, where I grew up, and wondering what people did in there. Faith was a gift that I hadn't received yet. Little did I know how much I'd find out later!

In college I focused on the sciences, and later I worked as a physicist. As I saw it, the real truth about the world and the origin of things, how things *really* were, was explained by science. Reality was explained by equations, so there was no need for childish things like religion. I didn't realize until later that there is no contradiction between science and religion.

My wife and I met on Cape Cod one summer when we were in college. I remember sitting on a dock with her when she asked me about my faith. I told her I didn't have any specific beliefs; it was that simple. Honestly, I don't know what Mary saw in me. But I know what I saw in Mary. There was a sort of inner glow to her, a real goodness about her, and I think it was because she was Catholic. I had never dated any Catholic girls before, and the difference I saw in her was very appealing.

We were married right after I got out of college, when we were twenty-two years old and Mary was still a junior. Mary's uncle was a priest, and he married us, despite the fact that I was a total nonbeliever. Since I'd never even been baptized, it wasn't a sacramental marriage.

Mary got pregnant soon after we were married, and the experience of having children brought her back to a fuller experience of faith. I had promised that we would bring the kids up Catholic; I was willing to do that. So when our daughters were baptized and Mary brought them to church, I went along; I wanted to be with them.

In fact, my desire for family unity led me to attend church every Sunday. One of the first times I went, an usher asked me to help take up the collection, which my wife and I thought was pretty funny. Going to church was actually very comfortable for me, surprising as that may seem. I don't know why, but I liked being there. So for twelve years or so we went on like that: all of us going to church together, despite the fact that I didn't believe in God. And twelve years of Mass going can have surprising effects, even on an atheist!

Our church had a program by which a couple would visit the family of a child who was about to be baptized and explain baptism. The nun responsible for the program asked my wife and me to be part of this, which seemed kind of strange. Sister explained that a lot of the couples were religiously mixed, and it would be useful for someone who wasn't religious to be part of the visiting couple for those people.

I think that, in her sneaky way, Sister helped me along my road to faith. I had to explain myself to these couples. God was on my mind; religion was an issue I couldn't escape. I wasn't a baptized Catholic, and in a way I wished I were.

For the entire twelve years, from the time I was married until the time I converted, my wife never once said to me, "I wish you were Catholic," or anything like that. She really didn't expect me to become Catholic; she loved me as I was. And leaving me alone was the best thing she could have possibly done. I never liked to be told what to do, and if she had tried to put pressure on me, it would have driven me away.

Instead my conversion just happened on its own. God did it. He is the one who converts hearts and souls. People can ask and pray, but he is the giver of faith.

Twelve years after we were married, the younger of my two daughters received her First Holy Communion. When my wife and daughters went up to take Communion, I felt left out. They were getting something that I wasn't, and I just knew I was missing out. I didn't believe, but I wanted to. For the first time I truly wished that I believed in God.

I guess that is where God saw his opening, because the next week I had a kind of religious experience that left no doubt in my mind. There were both physical and mental components to the experience.

The physical aspect is hard to describe; it was kind of like the shivers. There was definitely something real going on to get my attention, and it was accompanied by a mental awareness that sort of infused my consciousness. There are three things I remember being made aware of.

The first was that the Catholic Church was true. I had been sitting in church, listening to the liturgy and to the priests, for twelve years. I had been kneeling when I was supposed to kneel, standing when I was supposed to stand. I had been exposed to a lot of Catholicism for an atheist. And suddenly I was certain that it was all true.

The second thing was that God was real; I was utterly convinced of that. And the third thing, which was the most difficult for me to accept (given my previous unbelief), was that God loved me personally.

After going to church for all those years, I knew everyone in our parish, so I knew exactly whom to turn to when I needed instruction as a Catholic! I went through the Rite of Christian Initiation for Adults (RCIA), and at the Easter Vigil I was baptized and confirmed, and I received Holy Communion.

For the entire twelve years, from the time I was married until the time I converted, my wife never once said to me, "I wish you were Catholic," or anything like that. She really didn't expect me to become Catholic, but she loved me anyway.

One of the most beautiful parts of my story is that it doesn't end there. My whole family—including my parents and sister—used to go on vacations together. My sister is kind of an exercise freak, and so she'd always get up early and go for long walks. I like to get up early, too, so I'd often go with her. During this time together she asked me questions about my faith and what I believed. She became a Catholic, too, not long afterward.

This was hard on my mother. She and my dad still weren't religious, though they had come to the Easter Vigil Mass at which I entered the church. And now she had two children who were Catholics! She said to me, "There is a barrier between my children and me." I pooh-poohed it at the time, but it was true. There was a bond uniting me and my sister that she wasn't a part of.

I prayed for the conversion of my parents for seven years. I prayed to the Holy Spirit—seven Glory Bes, every day— kind of wondering how this conversion might come about. I always thought that it would be my father who would convert my mother, since my mother is the really stubborn one. But God's ways are not our ways, and it didn't happen like that!

My mother took RCIA instruction *twice* during those years to find out what I was up to. At the end of the two periods of instruction, she told me that she had two problems with the church. The first was contraception. She didn't say this, but I suspect that there was some personal reason for her resistance on this front. Maybe a family member had had an abortion or something.

The other stumbling block for her was the pope. My mother is a very independent woman; she doesn't like to be told by anybody what to do. So I think she was really bothered by the idea of being obedient to someone. But then she read *Crossing the Threshold of Hope* by Pope John Paul II, who was pope at the time. She said there was one page on which the pope was speaking directly to her. She figured he was either a fraud or for real, and she decided he was simply too wonderful not to be real.

At this point my father was very sick and clearly going to die soon. My mother wanted both of them to convert together; she wasn't going to do this alone. At an Easter party at our house, she went up to one of the priests who were there and said, "I need to become a Catholic!" He knew her well enough to know that she was serious and ready, and he understood the urgency behind the request because of my father's situation.

Father asked an associate priest, who was also at the party, to help my mom. We went right away to my father's room in the nursing home—my mother, me, my wife and children, and the priest. Both my parents were received into the church that day. My dad was close to death and couldn't speak much, but he had this wry smile on his face the whole time, as if he was surprised by this turn of events and happy about it.

I've been amazed by the outpouring of grace since my conversion. So many things have happened that have made the truth even clearer to me. For one thing, once I was baptized, my marriage became a sacramental marriage (between two baptized persons), and it changed for the better. It became more ordered, and we started receiving graces.

For example, I think that in a lot of families, once children come along the husband tends to be a bit passive. He tries to be the "good guy" with the kids, while the wife takes a more active role, dealing with the disciplinary needs of the children and so forth. It was that way in our relationship. I'd still be thinking about things while Mary was acting and disciplining. She resented the situation, and so did I, albeit in different ways. After my conversion this changed. Our relationship to our children and to each other improved tremendously.

Even in my work environment, the consequences of my conversion were phenomenally positive. I was no longer working as a scientist; I had gotten an MBA and was working for a company that was destined for some phenomenal growth. Our CEO was an evangelical Protestant who was sincerely trying to apply his faith to the workplace and was very positive about my religion. I became his chief of staff. Even though he was Protestant and I was Catholic, there was no tension between us: We built on what we had in common.

The CEO had a great perspective on and understanding of natural law; he saw that people are made in a certain way—for example, they seek to do good but are fallible. So he developed a beautiful way of running our company consistent with Christian principles. Leaders were encouraged to be servants to the people who worked for them. This led to some spectacular leaders and a place where people loved to work. I worked for twenty-seven years under this fabulously supportive CEO.

I've received so many blessings since my conversion. More than anything else, I have received the pearl of great price, the greatest gift you could be given. Everything has flowed from that.

One other moment that sticks in my mind, years later, is a dream I had, in which I was dying. Poison gas was in the air, and it was spreading out everywhere. I was trying to run away from it, but I couldn't run fast enough. Just as the gas was about to come over me, God swept me up in his arms, the way a father does with his children. I had this clear awareness that that's who God is—our loving Father—and that we will be swept up like children in our Father's arms when we die.

Most people wandering the earth don't have a clue of why they're here—which is really sad, since they're all children of God, loved by God their Father! A lot of people want things their flavor. But it's God who made things the way they are. We didn't make things up; he did. Anything that is false or man-made reveals its limitations sooner or later; you see the chinks in the armor eventually. That is not the case with our faith: It's rock solid.

I became like a sponge with the faith, soaking up everything Catholic I could get my hands on. I'm still like a sponge. The faith is really the only thing in this world that holds together and makes sense.

If someone tries to stump you with something, have no fear. There is always an answer. You may need to look for it, but it is there. I found that very comforting when I first converted—and still do.

Since my conversion it's been nothing but grace—in my family, my workplace, my life. And for that I will be eternally grateful.

CHAPTER SEVEN

—

Walking to the End

Karen Edmisten

Karen Edmisten is the author of The Rosary: Keeping Company
With Jesus and Mary *and* Through the Year With Mary: 365
Reflections. *A popular blogger whose work has appeared in
numerous Catholic magazines, she lives with her husband and
daughters in the Midwest.*

I have no idea how it happened.

I know the facts—the timeline, the steps. I know what I
wondered and wished for. But the *why* of it? How does one
analyze mystery or dissect love? Can I document the invisi-
ble and define what defies reason? How did I fall irra-
tionally, irreversibly in love with the God of rational, system-
atic, organized religion?

My conversion reminds me of something C.S. Lewis said:
"If you look for truth, you may find comfort in the end; if
you look for comfort you will not get either comfort or
truth, only soft soap and wishful thinking to begin, and in
the end, despair."[1]

Initially I *was* looking for comfort. But when the truth became enormously uncomfortable, I had to decide which path to follow, comfort or truth? I find it amusing (*now*—I didn't find it the least bit funny then) that God would use both my desperate unhappiness and my longing for truth to bring me to him. He used emotion *and* intellect, immanence *and* transcendence, attractions to faith *and* reason, to draw me closer. He's a complicated guy, but the result was simple: In looking for happiness, I found truth. And in embracing truth, I found happiness.

I was a pro-choice, anti-marriage, childless atheist because I believed these positions were right. I was pro-choice because I thought it was fair and compassionate. I was anti-marriage because it seemed the most sensible position. I was an atheist because I thought religion was weak and simple-minded, and atheism was the logical, intelligent conclusion about the nature of the universe.

I didn't care what anyone thought of me for holding my opinions. They had been formed through my personal lens and experience of the world. Others might see me as an immoral, callous, selfish, promiscuous baby-killer, but *I* knew I was none of those things. Compassion and love, common sense and logic, and a desire for an authentic, happy life were my principles.

The funny thing is, they still are. But now I'm a Catholic.

My earliest memory of religion is some kind of Sunday school: a classroom, robed and sandal-footed paper dolls. I asked my parents about it once, and they said they tried church but got nothing out of it. So I grew up in a house with Santa and the Easter Bunny but not the manger or the cross. Even so, I remember feeling as a young child that God watched everything I did and knew every one of my thoughts—an idea that was terrifying and exhilarating.

Religion didn't come up again until junior high school. A break in French class found a few of us chatting. Someone asked what religion everyone's family was. I panicked. Clearly, everyone was something, but what was I? I knew I wasn't Catholic, so I said, "Umm, we're Protestant." "Yeah, but what *kind?*" someone persisted. It was the first time I realized that we "weren't anything" by the standards of some.

My parents had their own kind of faith—faith in being kind, courteous, generous, and unselfish, faith in their family and in spending time with their friends. They believed in science and technology, not in the "fairy tales" of the Bible (as I once heard my grandmother call them) or the "Jesus Saves" variety of faith, which I had come to equate with all of Christianity.

One day my friend Cathy started dropping notes in my locker. "Jesus loves you," they said. I was annoyed. I didn't know Jesus, and I didn't want him chasing me. And I was decidedly opposed to Cathy butting into my non-relationship with him.

Cathy invited me out one night for pizza with her family. When we pulled into a church parking lot, I stiffened. She had not mentioned church. I was on high alert as we dug into the pizza. Then the night turned surreal. I couldn't believe that I was in a church hearing, "If you accept Jesus Christ as your personal Savior, come on down!"

The most shocking thing was that I was drawn. For a fraction of a second I considered what would happen if I stood up and went forward. I wanted the peace they promised, but I didn't understand how I could receive it simply by saying, "Count me in!" And if I was going to say yes to something, I had to understand it.

And there was the anger. Cathy had lied to get me there, and my fury at her trickery was stronger than my desire for the proffered peace. So I sat frozen. I went home unconverted and with the conviction that Christians were as deceptive as that serpent they chattered endlessly about. Sometime after that I realized that the presence I'd felt as a small child was gone.

Why, I wondered, had I been stupid enough to pray for truth if the truth was going to land me in the Catholic Church?

By the time I was in college, I was actively sculpting a worldview, piecing together a personal philosophy from the culture—from books, movies, friends, and experiences. Christianity I utterly rejected. The absurdity of it was confirmed by the people I saw around me. I was quick to condemn the hypocrisy I witnessed, marveling at the way so-called Christians got drunk, hooked up on Saturday night, then dutifully went to church on Sunday. I did the same things (minus the miraculous Sunday-morning rehabilitation) but took pride in being honest about what I did.

At a party one night, I saw a fellow student I'd overheard gossiping about me. With the emotional fortification of a large quantity of beer, I confronted her: "So, Deb,...I hear you think I'm a slut." She was horrified and embarrassed. Though I wouldn't admit it then, I relished shocking her; it was precisely the reaction I'd hoped for. So much for my own honesty, integrity, and lack of hypocrisy

I thought my life, unencumbered as it was by traditional morality, was one of enlightened, authentic freedom that would make me happy. But I found that my choices, so carefully designed to leave me carefree, left me drowning in misery. I was a more introspective person than I pretended to be, and my existential angst didn't mesh with my belief that life was meaningless but could be enjoyed. I began to see the world as a dark and hostile place. Virginia Woolf summed up my depression: "Why is life so tragic; so like a little strip of pavement over an abyss. I look down; I feel giddy; I wonder how I am ever to walk to the end."[2]

My self-made religion of freedom had backfired. I began exploring various belief systems as I tried to sort out what I believed to be right and true, but still I engaged in selfish and self-destructive behavior, deeply hurting people I loved. I finally quit college, utterly lost.

I kept returning to this: What is truth? If there was indeed a God who had created and who cared for the universe, where was he?

My friend Jack was inching his way back to the Catholicism in which he'd been raised. We talked frequently about his faith, but I had objections to just about every Catholic teaching Jack mentioned. At the same time I found examples of Catholic bravery around me.

I had a position in management in a marketing company, and I occasionally traveled to trade shows. On one trip a colleague and I didn't have a meeting until late Sunday morning. Still she rose early, showered, dressed in her prim navy blue suit, and made a phone call. Through the haze of a hangover, I asked her what she was doing. "Going to Mass," she said simply, keeping an eye out the window for her cab.

I had nothing to say. I wanted to find her ridiculous, but quite unexpectedly, I felt like the ridiculous one.

Shortly after that one of my fellow employees, a single woman in her twenties, became pregnant. She told me of her plans to put the baby up for adoption. As a Catholic, she said, abortion was not an option. I was stunned. It would have been easy to abort, to avoid letting a mistake ruin her life, to keep her business and her choices private. The fact that she cared so intensely about the baby she was carrying and about her religious beliefs touched me profoundly. And it shook me. What did *I* care that much about?

I started going to Mass occasionally with Jack. At his parish an enormous, exquisite wooden crucifix was fixed on the wall behind the altar. I remember staring at that man on the cross, aching to feel something, wanting to believe. But I didn't. Accepting Christianity meant losing myself, becoming something I was not. Self-surrender and obedience? Not for me.

I did wonder if a *little* Christianity might help—an idea here, a practice there, maybe some fasting. I could be kind to my neighbor, a little less snarky. But I didn't want the whole package. I still had many elementary questions, such as, "How do we really know this Jesus person even existed?"

This questioning period continued for a few years. I was graced with friends who patiently answered questions for me. They stuck with me as the questions became more challenging, as I asked for books and argued with them. They loved me even when I was thoroughly unlovable. And as I studied, read, processed our conversations, and loved my friends in return, something happened. Imperceptibly I began to believe in God the Father.

Could I call myself a theist? Maybe. Sorta. Kinda.

Then I read C.S. Lewis's *Mere Christianity*. It was revelation in a number of ways, but when I read that we can "hate the sin but not the sinner," I was stunned.[3] It was simple, but it settled so much.

For as long as I could remember, I had thought of my actions as *me*. They defined me. To condemn my actions was to condemn myself, and I had committed so much mortal sin (though I wouldn't call it that for a number of years) that to remain the "good and compassionate person" I assumed myself to be, I had to justify my actions. Professionals call it cognitive dissonance, and it was an enormous relief to release it. If God could separate what I had done from who I was, so could I. I fell to my knees and asked God's forgiveness for my many transgressions. I felt hope for the first time in many years.

But what about Jesus? I made two "mistakes" that are fatal to atheism. I read the Bible, and I started to pray, "Jesus, if you are God, show me."

One night I had a dream. I was fighting off a horrifying demon by repeatedly saying, "Jesus Christ—my Lord, my Savior—have mercy on my soul." When I awoke, choked and crying, I realized that I believed it. Jesus was my Lord. I was a Christian.

Not quite. If at one time I'd considered myself "too good" to be a Christian, I now knew painfully well that Jesus was far too good for me. I shunned the label "Christian"; I was unworthy.

One day a friend said, "Karen, there was one perfect Christian, and he died on the cross for you. Don't wait until you're 'good enough' to call yourself one."

He was right. It was time to get on with it. I began shopping for a church.

To an outsider Christianity is baffling. I thought there should be one church, with recognizable franchises all over the world. Neon signs and arrows indicating one had come to the right place would be helpful. Instead there were all kinds of indie operations calling themselves Baptists, Methodists, Catholics, Presbyterians. Why all the infighting? Though I assumed mainstream Protestantism was in my future, I had no clue where to start.

And while I was whining, why attend church at all? I preferred to pray in solitude. Couldn't I worship alone?

Further time in the company of C.S. Lewis convinced me that I needed to find *something*. The history of the Catholic Church held some appeal, but I simply couldn't imagine being Catholic. I spent a few months with a Lutheran church but moved on. I yearned for a denomination founded by Lewis; I'd be a devoted Lewisian. I settled on the Church of England, Lewis's church, which led me to Episcopalianism.

Episcopalianism boasted tolerance and none of the objectionable teachings of the Catholic Church. Its allure was powerful: ritual, liturgy, weekly communion, a sense of history. I felt, for a time, at home, sort of Catholic without the problematic messiness of Catholicism.

St. Matthew Episcopal Church was a serene and lovely place. The warm, friendly pastor welcomed me as a daughter. I chose to be baptized there. I was almost thirty years old.

By this time I'd been married several years. Tom and I had agreed on all the vitals before our wedding: a civil ceremony; no need for God in our lives; we'd never have children. My conversion was an unexpected, unappreciated alteration to the plan. Lazy Sunday mornings with coffee and the newspaper metamorphosed into fight scenes. Then came the wallop: I wanted a baby.

My poor husband. He hadn't signed up for any of this. I prayed that he'd change his mind about kids, and miraculously, his heart eventually softened. We tried to start a family, but our first two attempts ended in miscarriage. The way my faith sustained me through these griefs was staggering. If I had ever doubted the love of Jesus for me, I now clung to it as to a tangible treasure.

Finally our first daughter was born. But her birth and the radical changes in my life caused Tom and me to revisit past difficulties. Our marriage was in trouble. Concurrently, agonizing doubts caused me to leave the Episcopal Church. I was a denominational orphan, and the lack of worship was painful.

Jack gave me information about the Chaplet of the Divine Mercy and suggested I pray it every day. I did, and at the end of a month, Tom and I had resolved an enormous issue. I knew the chaplet wasn't a charm that invoked Catholic magic, but I saw the incident as another road sign on this perpetually surprising journey.

I still ached over the division among Christians and the lack of Christian companionship in my own life. I begged of God an answer, not to the question, "Where will I be comfortable?" but to the question, "Where is your truth?"

Jack and I continued to talk about Catholicism. I still had endless objections: the male priesthood, purgatory, closed Communion, Marian doctrines, confession, teachings on birth control, the pope and infallibility. I did admit *some* attraction. The Catholic Church seemed authentic in a way I couldn't (or didn't want to) articulate. But I didn't want to believe it could be the church that Christ established. I didn't want to admit I could have been so wrong.

Jack's explanations and recommended reading, however, toppled one objection after another. I was petrified. If the Catholic Church was the logical, sensible answer to my many questions, I'd have to become a Catholic. *No one* wanted that—not my husband, not family members, and certainly not I. But the more I read and prayed, the more sense it made: biblical arguments for all those "unbiblical" ideas, logic, consistency, a central church authority that hadn't wavered for two thousand years on essential teaching. Why, I wondered, had I been stupid enough to pray for truth if the truth was going to land me in the Catholic Church?

Tom and I were now living far from our old friends, and I didn't know a single Catholic in our town. But one Saturday evening, sweaty-palmed and with great trepidation, I went to a Mass. The bulletin announced RCIA classes were starting soon. Committed to nothing more than investigation, I signed up.

My first meeting was a disaster. I went home in tears, unsure of the validity of my marriage. I'd been led to wonder if I'd even be allowed to enter the church on my own, given my agnostic husband who wanted nothing to do with Catholicism. But I stuck with it, to find out what God had in store for me.

In those first months of regular Mass attendance, I felt conspicuous and lonely. Remaining seated while others received Communion, I wondered if they speculated about what horrible sin I'd committed that kept me in the pew. One week, feeling indignant, I got up and left after the Liturgy of the Word. It was painful for me to be in the presence of the Eucharist and be denied its healing power.

I complained to Jack of feeling like an outsider, not having a church community. He said, "But you do! Right now it's the community of inquirers." I thought, "*Great*, we're *all* outsiders." But the idea took root. There *was* kinship with others who were searching.

Jack also suggested I offer up feelings of isolation to God, that I think of remaining in the pew not as a judgment but as a fast from the Eucharist until I agreed with the Church on all issues. That made sense, and I decided to use that time to pray for the guidance I needed before I could, in good conscience, become a Catholic.

I continued to read the Bible, Christian history, and the early church fathers. Everything seemed to point to the Catholic Church. Family and friends were concerned I was making a huge mistake, but I felt God's guiding hand. I'd prayed repeatedly for him to lead me to the truth. Repeatedly he dropped me on the front steps of the Catholic Church. Maybe it was time to go in.

I had one more obstacle to overcome: the doctrine opposing birth control. I couldn't enter the Church and knowingly be unfaithful to one of her teachings. This brought me face-to-face with the core issue of Catholicism: the Church's teaching authority. I had to ask myself, "Did Jesus leave his

Church in the hands of the Holy Spirit or not? Does the Church have the authority to infallibly teach on matters of faith and morals?"

The apologetic and scholarly works of others much wiser than I had convinced me that the early Church wrote the Bible, and therefore the Bible could not, logically speaking, be our sole rule of faith. That made our other authority— our interpreter—the Church. Her teachings were not a pick-and-choose proposition, which meant I must be willing to submit to a teaching I didn't like or even fully understand.

Mark 10:15 tells us, "Whoever does not receive the kingdom of God like a child shall not enter it." *Like a child.* What does that mean?

What parent, when asked by her child, "*Why* do I have to do that?" hasn't at some time answered, "Because I'm the parent, and I said so." I realized that sometimes God asks me to do things I don't understand—because he's my Father, and he said so. I can pray and study to better understand difficult issues, but sometimes God calls me to obedience before he calls me to greater understanding.

After submitting to the teaching on birth control, it didn't take long for me to embrace it. I grew in knowledge and faith in this area perhaps more quickly than I had in any other. Living out the teaching has been an enormous gift to me, to my husband (who cooperated with it purely out of love for me and later converted to Catholicism himself), and to our marriage. Obedience brings God's grace, pouring over us in undeserved abundance.

Around this time I talked with Jack and said, "If I join the church at Easter..."

He said, "*If?* I thought you were ready."

"Yeah, but I still don't know everything about the Catholic Church."

"No one knows everything," he said gently. "If you wait until you're the perfect Catholic, it'll never happen."

Our talk echoed one from years before, when I'd waited so long to call myself Christian. God had proven to me that he loved me in spite of my messy, fumbling ways. And I desperately loved him. It was time to get on with it.

> Late have I loved you, O Beauty, so ancient and so new, late have I loved you! And behold, you were within me and I was outside, and there I sought for you, and in my deformity I rushed headlong into the well-formed things that you have made. You were with me, and I was not with you. Those outer beauties held me far from you, yet if they had not been in you, they would not have existed at all. You called, and cried out to me and broke open my deafness; you shone forth upon me and you scattered my blindness: You breathed fragrance, and I drew in my breath and I now pant for you: I tasted and I hunger and thirst; you touched me, and I burned for Your peace.
>
> —St. Augustine of Hippo, *Confessions*[4]

CHAPTER EIGHT

From Unbelief to Belief

Ken Krabbenhoft

Ken Krabbenhoft majored in Spanish and Portuguese at Yale University and went on to take a PH.D. at New York University in the same fields. He is now a professor at NYU. He lives outside New Paltz, New York.

> The times of martyrs come and go, but the time of witnesses never ends, and witnesses means martyrs.
>
> Madeleine Delbrêl[1]

In the late 1980s and early 1990s—before and after my fortieth birthday—I found myself moving from a fuzzy, complacent agnosticism into a deep spiritual crisis. My ongoing recovery from that crisis began with a sudden and unmistakable calling and the subsequent understanding and acceptance of the teachings of the Catholic Church. Along with several Catholic converts who gave me welcome advice and direction, the writings of the saints and doctors of the church reached across the years to play a crucial role in this transformation of my life. They provided me with a way out of the conflict and confusion that gave my passage into early middle age all the earmarks of despair.

A little background first. I was raised a Presbyterian in the suburbs of Detroit. Dad was usually at work, so it was Mom who carried through with religious education for me, my brother, and my sister.

As a teenager I began seriously examining questions of faith and morality, wondering if I might become a theologian. My idea of what that meant was pretty vague, something like sitting in a wood-paneled room reading Greek and pondering the nature of God. Our minister for Christian education, a graduate of Amherst and the Yale Divinity School, took me in hand. In addition to the rudiments of Calvinism, he helped me with New Testament Greek, which I figured I ought to know.

By my sophomore year in high school, I had found a niche in the youth group at our local church; the next year I was elected representative to the state youth synod. As gratifying as this was to my ego, however, I had no trouble abandoning it to go abroad for the second half of my junior year as an exchange student to Brazil. Taken from the coordinates I had known all my life and thrust into an environment almost unimaginably unlike the Calvinist Midwest—lifted from a Michigan February to my first encounter with saltwater and the tropical sun on the beaches of Rio—I found that my belief was socially rather than spiritually determined.

My Brazilian family and friends were humane and vibrant people without a shred of religious belief. They gave me the gift of a culture in which human contact, generosity, and the beauty of casual friendship were as highly valued as self-reliance, the solitary pursuit of knowledge, and strict adherence to the rules were praised back home. The fact that religious practice had no role in this did not trouble me in the least.

In retrospect it is difficult to encapsulate what Brazil meant to me without creating artificial dichotomies. Maybe it is enough to say that I felt my Brazilian friends had opened me to a broader and tremendously seductive sense of humanity—mine and other people's—which in the limited understanding of a sixteen-year-old stood in sharp opposition to Calvinism. (I'm tempted to say now, at age sixty-three, that Brazil's Catholic heritage is the root of that sense of humanity, however much contemporary Brazilians have abandoned the practice of Catholicism.) In short, I discovered that I wanted to be sophisticated, worldly, and pleasure-seeking rather than self-sufficiently pious.

It was also in Brazil that my love of languages and of literature flowered. By the time I returned home, these passions overshadowed Greek and religion. I thought of myself as a future novelist and critic, rather than a theologian. From high school I went to Yale, and by the end of my freshman year, I had ceased to have anything like a functioning Christian belief. Religion was a thing of my past, something I had "outgrown."

I knew I was a fraud and feared that the students knew it too. I saw with brutal clarity that someone like myself, who not only stood outside Christian tradition but lived a life that was fundamentally opposed to it, could not hope to do justice to the life of faith, let alone mystical practice.

In 1968 I married my college sweetheart and moved to New York City for graduate school at Columbia. Those were the Vietnam years, and I was a pacifist on purely secular and philosophical grounds. The government—bewildered, I think, by the extremism of my arguments—granted me exemption from the military provided I do alternate service, so I went to work for the welfare department.

In my spare time I tried to write fiction. Within a few years I had failed at this and failed at marriage. My wife left me in 1976.

I began drinking too much, floating from one temporary job to another and from one relationship to another. In the spring of 1977, Ferris Cook entered my life, and I enrolled in the graduate program at New York University. Ferris and I were married at the Manhattan Municipal Building in February 1979; our son Isaac was born in June 1980; and I defended my PH.D. thesis in Spanish and Portuguese literature in 1982. NYU offered me a job, and I have been there ever since.

God's healing grace, always sufficient, was at work all this time, despite the lack of cooperation from me, no less in my research than at home. In retrospect I see clearly how he led me to the Church through the topics of my doctoral dissertation—*kabbalah* (a form of Jewish mysticism) and Renaissance Platonism—and also through teaching the classics of Spanish Golden Age literature, including St. Teresa of Avila, St. John of the Cross, and playwrights like Tirso de Molina and Calderón de la Barca, who so brilliantly dramatized Catholic doctrine. In the same way, perhaps, that my family's Calvinism had introduced me to the universal truth of Christ crucified, my profession opened my eyes to the church's Jewish foundations and to the role of reason in clarifying and defending the faith. The spectacular achievements of Counter-Reformation metaphysics, jurisprudence, and moral theology inched me, bit by imperceptible bit, closer to embracing the magisterium.

Certainly none of this had a discernible effect on my spiritual life at the time: I didn't have a spiritual life, and how can something be influenced that isn't there? But the pagan compromise I had made with the world was being challenged by some of the greatest voices of the church. I may have given up on God, but God hadn't given up on me.

Fast-forward to February 1992.

One afternoon on my way to class, I found a student waiting for me in the hallway. This was a graduate class on the Spanish mystics, and I had been lecturing on the monastic reform movement initiated by Cardinal Ximénez de Cisneros in the late 1400s. Needless to say, I was teaching the course from the point of view of a nonbeliever with residues of Protestant bias. This meant that I could praise the originality of the mystics' style and the uncanny nature of their insights while ignoring or ridiculing such things as their belief in angels and demons.

As for what exactly happened at various stages of mystical prayer, all I could say was that it was a mystery. The best we could do, I told my students, was admire the brilliance of the mystics' rhetoric. We didn't have to pronounce on the truth or falsehood of their beliefs: We were students of literature, after all, not religion.

The student who was waiting for me was from upstate New York. She spoke Spanish with a thick Madrid accent that was

(I thought) almost comically at odds with her all-American looks. She told me that she had just gotten back from a retreat at a Benedictine monastery, and since we were discussing monasticism and prayer, would it be appropriate if she said a few words to the class about her experience?

I was a little concerned because I didn't know if her Spanish was *that* good (most of the other students were native speakers), but I thought it would be interesting to have an eyewitness account of what we had been reading about, so I invited her to speak briefly at the beginning of the class. The class would be two hours long: I figured I would have plenty of time to give my lecture after she had finished.

She started talking, describing the monks, the buildings they lived in, their schedule of daily prayer, the food they ate, and other details of their daily life. She used simple, direct language, and it was instantly clear that she spoke with complete honesty about a truth that she had grasped with her whole being, through experience. It was not just an intellectual or aesthetic exercise. I realized at once that, through her, God was speaking to me. He may have been speaking to the other people in the room too, but all I knew or cared about at the time was that he was speaking to me.

I understood quite clearly that, on the subject of mysticism, I had missed the point. The value of mystical writing was inseparable from the truth of mystical experience. What I had tried so hard to grasp intellectually could only be known through transcendent union with God. This, I allowed, was the great paradox of mystical literature: that it deals with something that words are inadequate to describe.

Up to this point I had failed to acknowledge that living a life in which *every act, gesture, and word* affirm the faith that can only come from God is different from living in consonance with moral law and the rational truths of theology. It is *never at odds* with this second, sacramental kind of living, which is the foundation of all spiritual life, but it is *nevertheless different* from it in the sense that it subsumes it and moves beyond it. Another way of putting it would be that some experience of the sacramental life was a prerequisite for even a superficial understanding of the Spanish mystics or any other mystics.

The student spoke for nearly an hour, and when she was finished, I picked up my lecture notes with a sense of shame. I knew I was a fraud and feared that the students knew it, too. I saw with brutal clarity that someone like myself, who not only stood outside Christian tradition but lived a life that was fundamentally opposed to it, could not hope to do justice to the life of faith, let alone mystical practice. I would go further now and say that pagans have no more right to teach and write about these things than grade-school children have a right to teach college physics.

I made it through the class on autopilot. It would be many years before I felt able to teach mysticism again.

Unbeknownst to my student, she had sowed a seed. The following winter, after taking Catholic instruction for nine months, I went on retreat to that same monastery—Mount Savior in Pine City, New York. I have been back many times since.

That day in February 1992 broke the shell I was encased in and pulled the cotton out of my ears. After half a lifetime of willful deafness, I was hearing what St. Teresa called "voices and callings" (*voces y llamamientos*). My student was the first of these; then, in quick succession, came a university colleague and her friend—both of them converts to Catholicism—and also her priest friend, Fr. James Halligan of St. Peter Church on Barclay Street, a block away from the World Trade Center.

St. Teresa said that these communications come to "those who have already begun to experience prayer" (*los que han ya comenzado a tener oración*). Why they should have come to me, who was not conscious of having any prayer life at all, is not a question I can answer. She also pointed out that these "callings" come to those chosen to receive them, not only from good people and sermons but "from things they read in good books" (*con palabras que oyen a gente buena u sermones u con lo que leen en buenos libros*).[2]

At this point you might be saying to yourself, "So far so good. In fact, a massive infusion of grace has enabled this man to take an honest look at himself for the first time in his adult life, to begin the spiritual recovery he mentions in the opening paragraph. The 'good people' and 'good books' God put in his way have given his intellect a mighty shove, knocking it out of the bumpy groove it had been locked into for over twenty years, imparting an impetus that moved it swiftly half-circle, to a position where it could challenge the *magisterium*, in good faith, as a preliminary to embracing the teachings of the Catholic Church in their entirety.

"But what about the crisis he speaks of? He wasn't aware that his understanding of the Catholic writers he taught was so flawed as to be fraudulent until that student spoke to his class. Was he also unaware that he was in the depths of a spiritual crisis? What exactly did this pagan life he refers to consist of?"

Let me speak about that crisis, because although at the time I wouldn't have been able to admit what later became so undeniable—that the root of my confusion and despair was spiritual—I nevertheless knew perfectly well that something was seriously wrong with my life.

In retrospect it is clear that I had reached what the twelve-step programs call a "bottom." That it was spiritual in nature was self-evident: I hadn't lost Ferris or Isaac (yet), I was a tenured professor (still), and I had an inventory of material possessions that many people only dream of, including a subsidized apartment in Greenwich Village, a country house and a car, work that took me abroad to countries I loved, the means to indulge my interests and whims, and so on. You might say that the world had rewarded me for my complacent compromise with its ways. But despite all these outward trappings of "success," I was miserable.

Ferris later revealed that she was on the verge of leaving me and taking Isaac with her. She loved me and knew that I loved her, but I had become next to impossible to live with. She didn't say it, but I knew that I was no longer the man she had fallen in love with.

When we met in 1977, I couldn't offer Ferris any of the things we had acquired in the interim. I was a thirty-one-year-old failed novelist with a seemingly unmarketable B.A.; I had a dead-end clerical job and was still legally married to another woman! But despite this, and despite the spiritual vacuum I lived in, Ferris and I were together, we were young and energetic, the future was before us. My passion for languages and literature was rekindling. Having emerged from the shattering self-doubt and rage of a marital breakup into the security of a love that by the grace of God would eventually prove to be truly sacramental, I felt a kind of hope for the future. It was a pagan variety of hope, so to speak; and even though I refused to see that its source was the God of Israel, we were happy, and we would soon be blessed with a son.

By 1992 the love was still there, but it had stopped growing. Everything else had changed. No longer young, no longer challenged professionally but coasting along a familiar road that led only to more of the same, no longer thrilled by the self-indulgent acquisition of things, sunk in a pit of self-absorption, I couldn't figure out what I had to live for.

Ferris, of course, felt this change more sharply than I did—than I *could*, rather, because my egotism and vanity had erected a barrier of denial between my conscience and my spiritual destitution. The prayers that Ferris (who has always considered herself a Christian) later told me she had offered on my behalf would be answered, but she had no way of knowing when or how. It never occurred to me to abandon her, but despair and desperation often go hand in hand. My mood swings betokened a deep psychological instability, and she had every right—maybe I should say, the self-protective *need*—to accept the possibility that I might go off the deep end. She had to shield herself and Isaac from my madness.

Of course, if you had asked me how things were going, I would have said, "Fine," because no matter how bad things had gotten, I still thought *I* could handle them, if only *I* could figure out *how*. That was the great contradiction: I *felt* I was powerless to change but *believed* I could solve my problems by myself. I was quite the expert on the subject of me, but that was the core of the dilemma: My own resources had been exhausted long ago, and I could no longer see anything clearly. There I squatted at the center of my universe, clutching the fine worldly credentials that I had by that time accumulated, immersed in intolerable despair, walled up against the deeper love that Ferris and I should have been growing into, shut off from the saving sacrifice of the cross.

As with Ferris, so with everyone else. My relationship with my son was marred by the demands I made on him to succeed academically and by my selfish impatience and prickly intolerance. The only person I could call a friend was my drinking companion, who was in pretty much the same shape I was. (As it turned out, he was the only person close to me who did not support my conversion and subsequent coming to terms with alcohol. I would have treated him the same had the roles been reversed.)

The journal I kept at the time was full of self-pity and fancied profundities. I went so far as to check the synoptic Gospels to see if the Greek word *elpis* ("hope") was found in quotations from Our Lord himself and was pleased to find, in effect, that it isn't. I came up with my own theological justification of this, nurturing a self-exculpating blame in my heart: If the Savior didn't think hope was worth speaking about, why should I torment myself for not having it? Forget about St. Paul and the rest of Scripture. By the terms of my diseased logic, I had made God himself responsible for my misery.

It was Fr. Halligan who gave me instruction and brought me into full communion with the Christian faith. I was received into the church on February 24, 1994, and confirmed on November 6 of the same year.

In the sixteen years since then, the embrace of the Eucharist, by which we give thanks to the Father for the Son's redemptive love, and the unending ministrations of the Holy Spirit have transformed my life completely. Where before there was the confusion, anger, and resentment of frustrated pride, there is now a semblance of clarity and, I think, an evolving detachment from those things that provoke the demons of my ego. Where before there was an assumption of entitlement that isolated me from the very people from whom I craved respect, there is now, it seems, the relative calm and growing acceptance of what it means to be just another of God's children, a worker among workers, a human being like any other.

This freedom to love and to be loved has reintroduced me to my vocation as husband and father and enabled me to learn something about friendship. My son, Isaac, took instruction shortly after I did, and we were confirmed the same day. Ferris and I were granted annulments of prior marriages and remarried in the church, a Catholic convert and a lifelong Episcopalian.

The Lord has blessed me with the grace to emerge from periods of doubt and stress with strengthened trust in him and the teachings of the church. I consider myself to be a productive member of society. I have not drunk alcohol in fifteen years. I am learning to have hope. I am happy.

On September 11, 2005, I traveled to the German town of Gettorf in Schleswig, not far from the Gelting Peninsula, where my surname, *Krabbenhöft*, originated. I went to Gettorf to see the church where my great-great-grandfather had been baptized, confirmed, and married prior to emigrating to the United States.

The church is a modest, late-medieval structure with a square bell tower; it is named after St. George—Sankt Jürgen in Low Saxon—and was the goal of a medieval pilgrimage in his honor. Construction began in 1318; the bronze baptismal font dates to the fifteenth century, as does the coat of arms hanging over a side door, emblem of the Counts von Ahlefeldt, masters of this entire area for almost six hundred years. Like most Catholic churches, over the centuries Sankt Jürgen accumulated testimonies to the devotion of its parishioners, including a chapel to St. George. Most of these would not survive the Reformation.

The first Lutheran sermon was preached there in 1523; the massive baptismal font was spared destruction, as was the exquisite 1510 carved wood altarpiece of Virgin and Child, but the St. George pilgrimage was banned in 1525, and the chapel demolished between 1610 and 1620. This part of Germany is still overwhelmingly Lutheran (87 percent), with Catholics accounting for a scant 6 percent of the population. The remainder are primarily Muslim or what I had been for most of my adult life: *Heiden*, atheists and agnostics (literally "pagans").

As I stood in the nave of Sankt Jürgen, in this land where my Saxon ancestors had abandoned paganism for the church of Rome well over a thousand years before, I felt, as a Catholic, that I had joined them, that I had reentered their tradition after a millennial hiatus. However mutilated, the Gettorf church was a focal point of the living past of my family—of my family's spiritual history—which reached out to me as someone who was, as Cardinal Newman put it, "deep in history."[3] Engagement with the "good people" and the "good books" of the Catholic Church put me back in touch with this history.

Gettorf was the last stop on a road that had led from Detroit to Brazil and Spain, from New Haven to New York City. But it was also the first step on a new road that led me from Rome to the birthplace of my father's fathers and the church they had dedicated, a long time ago, to a Catholic saint.

How did T.S. Eliot put it, in "East Coker"? "In my end is my beginning." I had come home.

CHAPTER NINE

─────

Conversion on Park Avenue
Mary Elizabeth

Mary Elizabeth is a former editor who now teaches religion full-time.

Shortly before I was born, in 1957, my mother was reading the society pages of the newspaper and came across the
name Mary Elizabeth, which I believe was a common Irish
Catholic name. Although she and my father had agreed to
name me Elizabeth, when the nurse in the hospital asked
her what my name was, she said, "Mary Elizabeth." When my
father heard this, he said, "Mary Elizabeth? What did you
name her *that* for?" As you will see, I think my name was sig-
nificant.

My father's parents were both half German and half
English, and their parents were from a combination of
Lutheran, Episcopalian, and Methodist backgrounds. On
my mother's side, my grandfather was from a Scotch
Presbyterian background, and my grandmother had
attended an Episcopal church as a girl, but neither of them
attended church as adults. While my parents have been

87

nonbelievers as long as I can remember, they had both been sent to Sunday school as children, and the culture that formed them in the 1930s and 1940s still reflected its Christian roots.

Both my parents cared deeply about the poor, and neither of them would ever have been deliberately unkind to anyone, although my father would certainly have gotten into a fight with a man if he was looking for one. My mother in particular was deeply concerned with being a good person and leading a moral life. Her and my dad's basic approach was that they didn't know whether or not God existed and probably thought it was impossible to know in this life.

I was not baptized when I was born. When I was six years old, my parents moved back to the town in northern New Jersey where they had both grown up and where all my grandparents were living. My father's mother soon began taking me to Episcopalian Sunday school, and I fell in love with God.

I asked my mother if there was a God. "Well...." she said doubtfully, "there's probably some *force*." I knew that meant no, or at least not the kind of God I had been learning about at Sunday school.

On a later visit to the church, I remember kneeling in the pew and praying to God, "You are all good and all wise, and therefore you know why I can't believe in you, and you won't be mad at me." I always felt that from that time, he never really let go—that he was quietly calling me, even when I refused to listen.

When I was about ten, I once argued with the other children in the neighborhood about whether or not there was a

God. I took the position that there wasn't, but as I walked home, I felt dissatisfied. Somehow it seemed that my family had gotten on the wrong side of this issue.

We attended an Episcopal church in Englewood, New Jersey, for about a year. My parents were still not interested in religion, but the pastor there was a charismatic man whom a lot of people found inspirational and helpful, so we went. The church itself was unusually beautiful, and I was fascinated by it from the moment I entered its doors, as well as by the large crucifix that hung from its rafters. Most of the liturgy was a mystery to me, but I would sit and study the crucifix and think about what it meant.

I was also deeply impressed by some of the stories from the Old Testament. I understood that if you loved God, you had to be willing to suffer to prove that you loved him. Although we stopped going to the church when I was only ten or eleven, it had made a deep impression on me.

In my freshman year of high school, I became very unhappy in public school. I asked my parents if I could attend a progressive high school in Greenwich Village that I had heard about. My parents' politics were liberal, and they agreed. The philosophy of progressive education encouraged students to say what

I told the admissions officer that I was interested in combining the fields of history and psychology and studying, in particular, the rise of the cult of the Virgin Mary in the Middle Ages— from a strictly scientific point of view, of course. This greatly impressed the admissions officer, and to this day I believe that Our Lady was responsible for my being accepted at Yale.

they wanted to study, and I asked the school to give us classes in both religion and Latin, having picked up from my reading of Jane Austen novels that educated people knew Latin.

My girlfriends and I (all from secular families) became quite excited about the prospect of attending the religion class. We were finally going to get to the bottom of this religion thing. However, the teacher proved to be a former nun who was dressed in a very masculine way, which we had never seen before. (This was the mid-seventies.) She was clearly quite hostile to our interest in religion. She more or less growled, "What do you want to know?" That was enough to shut us all up. After that class we never asked for another, and I suspect that the school administration was relieved.

But religion was a subject that continued to draw me. I developed an interest in Jungian psychology because of its focus on religious symbolism. While I thought Christianity was not true, I pursued ideas and movements that seemed to have at least some connection with it, including Communism.

We did not have grades at our high school, so I was surprised when the guidance counselor recommended that I apply to Yale. I told the admissions officer that I was interested in combining the fields of history and psychology and studying, in particular, the rise of the cult of the Virgin Mary in the Middle Ages—from a strictly scientific point of view, of course. This greatly impressed the admissions officer, and to this day I believe Our Lady was responsible for my being accepted at Yale.

In the spring of my freshman year, I took a class entitled "Introduction to the New Testament." Having no knowledge of religious studies, I thought the class would explain the basic beliefs of Christianity. Instead the course focused on the work of German Scripture scholars, such as Rudolf Bultmann, who believed that much of the New Testament was derived from the mythologies and stories of the cultures surrounding the Jewish people. I can't recall that this theory was ever backed up by any concrete evidence; I don't think any of the essays that we read for the class ever gave a specific instance of an incident or parable in the New Testament that came from another culture or religion. But the implication was that Christianity was not true.

That spring I consciously thought about whether or not God existed. Given my studies, it seemed to me more likely that he did not exist than that he did, and this thought created feelings of despair in me. One day, as I was sitting at my desk in my room, I said to myself, "I will never know if God exists, and it is too painful to think about it, so I'm not going to think about it anymore."

Soon after this resolution, I fell deeply, madly in love with a boy who was a senior at Yale. Unfortunately, he turned out to be mentally ill, and I was heartbroken when the relationship ended nine months later. On the rebound I became involved with another undergraduate, a Russian émigré who had come to the States at the age of sixteen and was at Yale on a full scholarship. I had continued to study Marxism in college; now I was in a relationship with a man whose family had fled the Soviet Union.

My boyfriend occasionally talked to me about the Soviet Union, but I mostly ignored him. Then I read a book his father had written, a brilliant account of his life under Stalin that was lavishly praised by Robert Massie in the *New Yorker*. The book had the kind of impact that Solzhenitsyn's *Gulag Archipelago* might have had. I went from thinking that the Communists cared about the poor to thinking that Communism was hell on earth. Knowing the author personally made the book even more persuasive.

This perspective made me a bit of an outsider at Yale. It was the late seventies, and some of my fellow English majors were traveling to El Salvador and Nicaragua to take part in the revolution. I now regarded mainstream political and cultural opinion with suspicion, a fact that probably helped set the stage for my conversion: Since I now distrusted the views of elite opinion makers, their rejection of Christianity was less important to me. In retrospect I think my fear of being different from other people and being rejected by my peers before my conversion was much stronger than I realized at the time. But now that I was anti-communist, I was already different, so becoming a Christian was less daunting.

In my third or fourth year at Yale, I finally learned the basic Christian story by reading Milton's *Paradise Lost* for one of my courses. For the first time I understood the Christian notion of sin in a general way, and I began to pray interiorly for forgiveness. For one thing, I felt that it had been wrong of me to enter into the relationship I was currently in when I had still been in love with someone else.

I also remember thinking during this time that if I became a Christian, I would have to give up my boyfriend, because Christianity taught that sex outside of marriage was wrong. I was very emotionally dependent on my boyfriend and couldn't imagine life without him. I didn't realize that if I became a Christian, God would give me the support I needed, both through my relationship with him and through the friends that he would bring into my life.

At the end of three years, my boyfriend and I broke up in a very painful manner. At the very same time, my best friend from high school died of cystic fibrosis. When I was told over the phone of her death, I was seized with the desire to find a church.

It was a cold, dark, rainy September night. I ran from one Protestant church to another on campus, but they were all locked up. Suddenly I remembered that there was a Catholic Church nearby.

It felt a little spooky going into the church, as though I was entering the twilight zone. I hadn't realized the degree to which prejudice against the Church had affected me on a subconscious level. I knew nothing about the Blessed Sacrament, but I knelt down and said the only prayer I knew, the Our Father. (Several months later, on a train to New Haven, I sat across from a woman who worked for that church. When I told her that I had gone to the church at night to pray, she told me that the church was always kept locked in the evening.)

After I left the church that night, I returned to my room with the inner conviction that God existed. I decided, however, that I wouldn't tell anyone. I didn't want to be considered a "Jesus freak." My conviction that God existed soon wore off though. I wanted Christianity to be true; I thought it was the only thing that could comfort me. But I was not at all sure that it was.

After graduation I returned to the New York area. My best friend, the woman who had died, had gone to St. Hilda's school, near the (Episcopal) Cathedral of St. John the Divine. I would visit the cathedral and weep for my friend, but to avoid the other people there, I moved to a side chapel that happened to be devoted to Mary. I would sit in front of Mary's statue and weep, only because the statue was there. Despite the comments I'd made to the admission officer at Yale, I really didn't know much about Mary.

I found a job as a newspaper stringer, a sort of cub reporter, at the *Bergen Record*, which was my hometown paper, located in Hackensack, New Jersey. I became close friends with the oldest person in the newsroom, a twice-divorced Catholic. He wasn't going to church, but he knew what I was looking for. One night in the parking lot, he taught me the Hail Mary. Since the only other prayer I knew was the Our Father, I began to say the prayer occasionally.

Several months later I got a job at *National Review*. For the first time in my life, I met intellectuals who were Christians. One girl there, who became a very good friend, was a devout Catholic. The daughter of a fireman, she was a brilliant young woman who by eighth grade had read every book by C.S. Lewis, G.K. Chesterton, and the founding editors of *National Review*. She had an intellectual sanity, a clarity about life, that I had never encountered before. She was very cautious about pushing her faith on me, and oddly, we never discussed religion.

I had been visiting various mainstream Protestant churches, looking for a spiritual home. However, I was only interested in Christianity if it was true, and the churches I visited seemed to have little faith. One famous church in Brooklyn Heights, where I was living, had an illustrious past, but on the second visit, the minister gave a sermon about how abortion was morally acceptable. I didn't know what to think about abortion, but I knew that if the God of the New and the Old Testaments existed, abortion was a grave offense against the moral law. I never went back.

One denomination in particular I perceived as being for the upper class. I liked the good things that went with that—beautiful churches and liturgies—but I thought it was a little disingenuous to become a Christian and a member of this denomination at the same time. I felt that the Catholic Church was for everyone, and that fact made it seem authentically Christian. In addition to my friendships with Catholics, it was really that thought that pushed me in the direction of the Catholic Church. I didn't know that *catholic* meant "universal."

After I had known my Catholic friend for a year, she gave me two books by C.S. Lewis for my birthday: *Surprised by Joy* and *The Four Loves*. After I read them I went to her and said, "I want to talk to a priest." I still can't believe those words came out of my mouth. But I think deep down everyone knows that the priest is close to God. My friend found a wonderful priest for me to talk to, and I met with him occasionally over a two-year period.

During this time I read Christian apologetics and the Gospels, and I was praying and thinking about the faith. I still wasn't sure that Christianity was true, but I now believed it was more likely to be true than not. The highly intricate order and beauty of the world made it difficult to believe that creation had come into existence by chance. I also found it hard to believe that matter was able to organize itself in such a way as to produce human consciousness. Human love and great art pointed to the probable existence of a soul.

And then there was Judaism: If Christianity wasn't true, had the Jews made up God? There were certainly strange things in the Old Testament that I didn't understand, but there was something authentic and true about the Psalms and the other writings.

Finally, there were the Gospels. As Christian apologists have been pointing out from the earliest centuries of the Church, if Jesus wasn't telling the truth about himself, he was either mad or evil. How could someone who was mad or evil be the source of the most beautiful moral teachings the world has ever known? If the apostles had made up the Gospels, not only were they literary geniuses, but they had died for something they had fabricated.

Nonetheless, I still didn't have certitude, and that's what I wanted before I converted. I didn't realize that certitude was a gift that one receives at baptism.

One day as I was reading the Gospels, I came to the passage where Jesus said, "Ask, and it will be given you; seek, and you will find; knock, and it will be opened to you" (Luke 11:9). I got down on my knees in my room and said, "OK, Jesus, I am asking, I am seeking, I am knocking: Give me faith."

I began attending Mass on Sundays at a church a block from my apartment on the Upper West Side of Manhattan.

I would sit in the back of the church during Mass and ask for the gift of faith.

Finally I asked the priest with whom I had been talking to meet me for lunch at a midtown restaurant. Over lunch I explained to him why I couldn't possibly believe in God, raising all my strongest objections to the faith. He had very strong answers, although I wasn't completely convinced by them. I left the restaurant happy that Christianity might be true.

And then, as I was walking up Park Avenue toward my office, I had a mystical experience—an ecstasy. I felt as if the heavens were opening up and I might start to levitate. I felt that I was madly in love with God, and he was madly in love with me. It was the same feeling I had had when I fell in love in college, only a hundred times stronger. St. John says, "God is love" (1 John 4:8), and when God manifests himself, we feel bathed in that love.

A businesswoman was walking toward me, carrying a briefcase. I wanted to run over to her and tell her that everything was going to be all right. I believe that I was given the gift of faith on that day.

Some years later I came across the date on which I had met the priest for lunch. It was September 8, the day Catholics celebrate the birth of the Blessed Virgin. I think that was Our Lady's way of showing me that it was she who had obtained the gift of faith for me.

Looking back, there were three major factors that enabled me to respond to God's grace. The first was the depth of my suffering. If I hadn't needed God so badly, I probably would not have persisted in my search for him. Second was my intellectual distance from mainstream opinion. Third was the great gift of Catholic friends. While many people become Catholic without this grace, I think for me it was crucial.

In the months leading up to my decision to be baptized, God sent two wonderful Catholic friends into my life, in addition to my friend from *National Review*. (One of these young women eventually entered a convent.) They in turn introduced me to several other Catholic friends, who were among the most refined, cultured, and fun people I had ever met. So I had a world of Catholic friends that I wanted to belong to.

My faith has continued to be tremendously important to me since my conversion twenty-six years ago. Certainly the faith gave me peace and a stability I had never known before. My life has not always been easy since that time—there have been many trials and temptations—but I have had the joy of knowing that my faith is real.

———

CHAPTER TEN

From *Cantus Firmus* to *Terra Firma:*
His Beauty Drew Me
Jonathan Fields

Jonathan Fields trained as a musician at Yale and the Mannes School of Music. Since then he has worked professionally as a musician in various capacities, particularly in advertising and religious music. He lives in Brooklyn with his wife, Susan, and their three children.

I grew up in Westchester County, New York, one of three kids. My home life was very Jewish, but there was no religion, no belief in God in our home. I don't know if my parents were really hard-core atheists, but we never talked about God. Their worldview was essentially Freudian and vaguely socialist.

At the same time my parents weren't ideologues, so there was a kind of humor to their perspective, a lively, Jewish wryness to their attitude. They were secular enough that we celebrated Christmas, not Hanukkah, but naturally there was no religious element to it. There was, however, a real love of knowledge in our home. Art and beauty were very important to us—especially to my mother. We had some pictures of the Virgin Mary around the house, because my mother thought that the Madonna was a beautiful image of motherhood.

Around the age of eleven or so, I began to realize that being Jewish meant being different from other people. Every so often I'd get called "Jew boy" or something like that, and I'd realize that, even without religion, I was part of a people that are somehow set apart. I asked my parents if I could be bar mitzvahed, because I wanted to know more about who I was and about the people I was a part of. So I went to Hebrew school, and I started to think about myself in a deeper way. I was searching for my identity and looking for answers to questions I didn't know how to put into words yet.

My father loved music, so I grew up listening to the classical and jazz music that he would often play. I especially remember the Beethoven symphonies and Miles Davis. At a certain point in high school, I got really into music. I was very passionate about it, very intense and driven in my exploration and dedication to both playing and listening.

Around the same time I realized that there was a deep sadness in me that I didn't really know how to explain.

The people I knew explained things with Freudian answers—the unconscious and so forth—but I sensed that my unrest went deeper than that. I didn't really buy these answers to my questions; I think not even my parents did. Freud didn't explain things to me; Marx seemed somehow superficial; nothing I learned about seemed to speak to who I was and how I could understand myself, what I felt and why.

My search for answers took off in music. I was truly moved by the blues; they spoke to the sadness I had inside. I sensed in that music an answer greater than the psychological and political explanations I had gotten up to that point.

As I look back, I see that there were things even then that led me on the path to Christ. I wasn't the stereotypical "Jewish kid"; I hung out with the poor kids and ——— poked fun at the excesses of liberal ideas—even though I mostly agreed with them. I even took a part-time job tuning guitars for the folk Mass at our local Catholic church.

In that music I saw something that the faith could give me, something more beautiful and truer.

After high school I started college at Yale. The teachers I had there were pretty insignificant on my path, but I remember hearing Stravinsky and Mozart for the first time through friends I met there. Mozart amazed me: There was such a beauty and such an order to it; I wanted more of that.

After a little while at Yale, I got very sick. I had a bleeding ulcer, and I almost died. When I recovered I had a strong sense that God existed—I don't know why. I had been curious about religion before, but now that I intuited there was something greater out there, I got more interested. People suggested various books to me, particularly Buddhist stuff; someone gave me *Zen and the Art of Motorcycle Maintenance.*

Yale was too much for me though. After my sophomore year I transferred to Mannes School of Music in New York. There I learned about everything related to music. And much of it led me to the Church.

I started studying counterpoint, the juxtaposition of two very different musical lines that form one harmonious whole. The first time I heard *cantus firmus* ("fixed song"), of which Gregorian chant is a type, I realized that there could be a solidity as well as an order to things. I didn't know yet that this came from the church.

I was struck by the fact that music was more than personal expression, more than being a superstar. It wasn't about being the next Jimi Hendrix; there was something bigger and deeper than that. I saw something in music that the faith could give me, something more beautiful and truer than what I'd seen up until then.

At Mannes I learned about Dante, St. Francis, and everything connected with the Order of the Mass. While reading a book by a theosophist, I had a revelation, and I accepted Christ as the Messiah. From there I tried lots of different religions. But my education in music kept bringing me back to the church. I found the beauty of the Mass particularly moving.

My roommate was Catholic. (He was marrying a Muslim woman and was struggling with a lot of things.) One day I went to his church, walked upstairs to the balcony, and joined the choir. Six months later I became a Catholic.

My education in the faith was terrible though; I really knew nothing. And then I had to tell my parents about my conversion. That was very hard for them; they couldn't understand it. While they were quite secular, they strongly identified with their Jewish heritage.

I became very isolated at that point, cut off from pretty much everyone I knew. It was a confusing and excruciating time. Being alone took a psychological toll on me, and I didn't want my parents to think that my religious decision was the result of a psychological problem. I had a tremen-dous religious zeal, and I really wanted to give myself to Christ, but I was also having some really serious problems with depression. I was constantly convicting myself for my sins—very intense, wild stuff—and I was afraid of the devil. At one point I was very near to a nervous breakdown, though I didn't realize it at the time. I finally went up to St. Jean Baptiste in Manhattan and talked to some of the priests there; they took me under their wing and were very good to me.

One Sunday morning I woke up feeling overwhelmed with an awareness of my loneliness. I felt isolated in the church; it seemed as if most of the people there didn't truly believe in Jesus, that they weren't there with their whole selves. In desperation I went to a phone book and started looking for pro-life people. I knew that there was something essential to the faith that was alive in the pro-life movement. I figured these people had to really believe in Jesus.

I found the name of a lady who was head of the Right to Life branch in Westchester County, and I called her. She said, "Well, there is this priest, Msgr. Wrenn, you could talk to." So I called him, and he told me to come and see him immediately at Our Saviour Church.

I was a mess: I hadn't eaten, I hadn't shaved, and I hadn't slept in two weeks. But Msgr. Wrenn listened to my story very seriously. He told me, "I know what you need: You need to talk to a friend of mine." He called a psychologist friend, Paul Vitz, and arranged a meeting. "First though," Msgr. Wrenn told me, "you need to go home and clean yourself up. Get a shower, shave."

I had always done things on my own, but I could see that I needed more than what I could give myself. I knew that I needed to listen and do what Msgr. Wrenn suggested. It was then that I learned to follow.

I went to see Dr. Vitz only a couple times, but it changed my life. He recommended that I see a great parish priest named Fr. James Halligan, a very simple, very good man. He was very kind to me, and he helped me tremendously. He was living at a sort of pre-seminary in New York at the time, and he arranged for me to stay there. People thought I was just another guy discerning a vocation.

Fr. Halligan encouraged me to see my parents again, and he even drove me to their house. My parents started to see that my faith was part of me and something they had to accept. Little by little my life was coming back together.

Father also helped me see that I was having a nervous breakdown. Dr. Vitz encouraged me to get out of my isolation. He told me not to stay home alone, and he suggested that I go to a meeting of Communion and Liberation (CL) in my area. CL is a movement within the church that stresses the personal nature of the encounter with Christ and has a strong community dimension. Dr. Vitz told me I would find real friends there.

The movement[1] became a central part of my life very quickly. There was—and is—a sense of a people in CL, a sense of being part of a community that is the church. This made me feel human again. It actually reminded me in many surprising ways of the kind of life I had growing up. There were four families that we were close to and with whom we did everything: We would go on vacation together and look at all the aspects of our lives together. Life in the movement was similar.

When I had first become Catholic, there was always a tension in my mind about what it meant to convert as a Jew. I wanted to be sure that I wasn't renouncing my heritage; I had to know that what I was doing was consistent with who I was as a Jewish person. My involvement with CL made it clear to me that converting wasn't a rejection of my identity so much as a fulfillment of it. I had found the same sort of community that my parents always had. Christ hadn't changed the method that God established with the Jewish people.

I have now been Catholic for over twenty years; I am married and have three children. My parents and I have a very strong relationship. They see that in my conversion I have found a community that loves me and my family—and them as well.

The Catholic community is a really important part of my recognizing Christ's presence in my life. Through people in the church I have become aware of the tremendous mercy of Christ. When I was first converting, I was really bowled over by the beauty of the Catholic faith, and I was especially moved by the stories of the Prodigal Son and the woman caught in adultery. The experiences of the son and the adulteress have become more and more my own reality. I see that my deepest need is to be forgiven and loved, and that is what has happened—and what continues to happen. These tremendous and beautiful experiences don't go away, and they make me see that the one who started this action in my life is still with me and acting in it.

Today I still struggle with many of the weaknesses and failings I always have. I think that without the faith, I would give in to a kind of despair. But now I know that my difficulties in life are part of a greater plan.

Jesus gives me this certainty of being loved unconditionally. This makes me sure that what I've found is the true faith, and it's for everybody. Everyone has the hope of being loved as I've been loved. I see the same needs in the eyes of people sitting on the train on the way to work in the morning. My deepest hope is that they can one day know the mercy of Christ the way I do.

CHAPTER ELEVEN

Discovering Truth—and Unconditional Love
Olga

Olga was born and raised in Warsaw, Poland. In the middle of the 1980s, she moved with her parents to the United States. After graduating from college in 1994, she worked as a computer programmer. She is now a wife and home-schooling mother of three children living in Pittsburgh. She entered the Catholic Church during Easter of 2000.

T he primary reason I was an atheist was simply because I had been born and raised in a family that had no belief in God. I was born in Warsaw, Poland, in 1971, during the Communist period, and while my father was Jewish by ethnicity, he was a nonbelieving atheist. My mother had been born in Russia and baptized in the Russian Orthodox Church, but her family had never practiced the faith in any way. Both of my parents had obviously been deeply influenced by the atheistic Communist culture of their countries, in which a good citizen was expected to rarely speak of religion except as a distraction for people.

My worldview was simply that of a young girl who believed what her parents told her. The teaching I received was that the religious stories people believed in, such as those written in the Bible, were simply primitive superstitions that were no longer needed in the modern era of scientific understanding. Religion was only for the narrow-minded and unsophisticated people of the world. My father constantly reminded me of the Catholic Church's supposed participation in the Holocaust and of the anti-Jewish sentiments that the church supposedly held. This thinking encouraged my own feelings of distrust toward the Catholic Church.

While I wasn't an ardent atheist, I simply didn't think much about the spiritual. I took it for granted that God probably didn't exist. This was the paradigm I inherited, and it is the worldview I held well into my twenties.

Meanwhile my family life was basically good but not very rich in relationships. This left me oftentimes feeling lonely. I had a sister who was much older and very distant, and our parents were very much into comparing us with each other and our friends. Both of us felt that we weren't measuring up in their eyes. There was a lack of acceptance of who we were and an overall sense of inadequacy and pessimism that dominated family life. This pessimism, which I see now was at least in part due to the lack of a faith life in my family, was something that I took into my adulthood.

My awareness that the atheistic view was inadequate happened gradually. I see now that the seeds of it were planted even when I was a child in Poland. I had this longing for someone to love me just for who I was. I recall thinking that if there was a God, I did indeed want to feel his love and acceptance. I am not even certain where I picked up this notion of a loving God, but a desire to feel loved in such a way was most definitely in my heart.

Perhaps this notion came from my interactions with my friends in Catholic Poland. My most exceptional friends seemed to come from the practicing Catholic homes. Those children accepted me and were always friendly to me, no matter what my beliefs were. On some occasions they were unable to spend time with me because they had to go to Mass. It's funny now that they often envied me because I didn't have to go. But I sometimes accompanied them at Mass. My parents would *not* have approved, but I felt that what they didn't know wouldn't hurt them.

On one occasion my mother found a beautiful gold necklace with a medal of Mary holding the infant Jesus, and she gave it to my sister. I vividly recall sneaking the medal from my sister's room and using it to pray to God. In tears I asked him to make me feel loved. This first attempt at praying was strange, for it seemed odd to hope that someone was listening to my prayers. But while it took twenty years, that prayer was indeed answered.

During my adolescent years I didn't give much further thought to religion or to God. It was during this time that my family emigrated from Poland to the States. Even as a newcomer, I became busy with the things that teenagers are

I saw my husband changing in profound ways. He was becoming a better husband! He became a better listener, more thoughtful and caring, more humble and loving. I began to realize that if being Catholic could change him in this way, there might just be something to it.

typically busy with—fitting in, trying to look pretty and be popular—and there was little time for or inclination toward deeper thinking.

One thing that does stand out for me is a deep sense of sadness that pervaded my life, especially during my later high school years. As an immigrant I had a difficult time making deep friendships, and because my family was not connected to a faith community or an ethnic community, I had little chance to connect with people with whom I had much in common. This left me feeling very isolated and lonely most of the time.

During college I began dating the man who would become my husband. My relationship with him has had the deepest impact on my life and on my conversion. Steve had been a cradle Catholic, and later an evangelical Christian, but had stopped going to church, and he became more or less an agnostic during our dating relationship. We were both young when we married, only a few years out of school, and we were mostly focused on careers, making money, acquiring things, and generally seeking and living the pleasurable life.

Several years into our marriage, Steve began to feel a deep sadness. One day he tearfully told me that me that he was not happy with his basically secular life, that it felt empty. I couldn't disagree, as I felt much the same. Despite all the outward appearances of success, we both sensed a lack of meaning, and neither of us had even begun to find happiness.

Steve realized that something was missing from our lives, and he felt that something was God. After a lot of thought and prayer, he told me that he was going to start searching for God again—even if that meant he would have to go back to church. He knew that I might oppose that, but he felt he had no choice. He was being called to search for the truth. He said he would be very happy if I would join him, but he knew it would be difficult for me.

At that point I asked myself, "What now?" What new fad had he come up with? I suppose I could have said that I was not going to support this, but we had been friends for about ten years, and I felt that he was indeed my best friend. I did have a desire to always be by his side.

I also thought back to when I was a girl going to church with my friends. If I could go with them then, why wouldn't I go with Steve now, even if just to keep him company? It was not as if I would have a big sign on my head that said, "Beware: Atheist!"

Before we even got to the point of going to church though, Steve began to read and study everything he could about religion—from Islam to Hinduism, to Mormonism, to Judaism. He discussed much of what he read with me, but I wasn't really that interested. Through this long period of study, he eventually felt drawn back to the faith of his child- hood. He decided to start practicing Catholicism.

And then I saw my husband change in profound ways. He became a better husband! He became a better listener, more thoughtful and caring, more humble and loving. This drew me toward a more open attitude toward the faith. I realized that if being Catholic could change Steve in this way, there might just be something to it.

I began to attend Mass and converse with my husband about what was going on. I realized how little I really knew about the Christian faith or even about the Jewish faith of my father's heritage. As I learned about Catholicism, my objection on the basis of its anti-Semitism began to break down. I learned that Christianity and Judaism had a common history. I heard the Old Testament read at Mass, and I learned that the prayers of Jesus were directed to the same God as were the prayers of the Jews. This was important to me, because although my father and I had never practiced Judaism, I still felt an ethnic affinity toward it.

Equally important were other messages I received at Mass that I'd not heard before—messages about openness and loving others. The atmosphere in church, far from being condemning and closed-minded, was inviting to anyone with a heart to hear. Sometimes I was touched to the point of tears as I drank in messages about self-sacrifice, loving service, forgiveness, and so much more. I started to feel truly thankful that my husband had come back to church and brought me along with him. These experiences made me question the negative things I had heard about the Catholic Church.

Once I began participating in the life of the Church and going to Mass, I became more self-aware, and (as with my husband) I began to be changed in profound ways. I now had a way to check my behavior against a real standard, the standard of love. Has what I've done hurt others? Is what I've done in line with what Mary would do, in line with what Jesus would have me do?

This slow but steadily growing participation in the faith culminated in my coming into full communion with the Catholic Church at the Easter Vigil in 2000. Despite many fears and doubts that I still had, I was able to humble myself and, for the sake of unity with my husband and for the sake of my then four-month-old baby boy, I decided to undertake the life of faith and do my very best to walk as a faithful Catholic.

I continue to be presented with the truths of the faith, which remind me that I am not walking in darkness but in the light of Christ. And while the standard seems very high—Jesus, after all, is the perfect Son of God—the Church acknowledges that we are imperfect human beings and even offers us a sacrament to reconcile with God when we make mistakes. This brings me great peace. I don't have to beat myself up over my mistakes. All I need to do is humble myself and ask for God's forgiveness in order to begin again becoming the person God wants me to be.

Ultimately it is the hopefulness of Catholicism that resonates very deeply within my soul. And there is the realization that God's existence makes everything we do matter, that life has true and everlasting meaning. God has placed us in this world for a reason, and everyone in this world is special to God, no matter how old or young, healthy or sick, rich or poor. We are important simply because God created us and loves us. And because he loves us, he gives us opportunities to grow in spirit and to learn to love him and others unconditionally.

Before I became a Catholic, life at times seemed meaningless. My success was derived from fleeting things of the world such as career, possessions, and outside approval. I was taught that if I was not successful in these areas, my life would be a failure, and I would be humiliated, less valuable as a human being. Career and material possessions no longer define me as a person. I feel special in God's eyes no matter what mistakes I make.

Why am I Catholic? Because the heart and soul of what the church teaches resonate with what my heart and soul long for: faith, hope, and love. Because I have found that the message of forgiveness and renewal, even through suffering and self-sacrifice, is true in my life and in the lives of those I love. Ultimately what converted me, and continues to convert me, is the fact that the faith proves itself to be true in the living out of it.

NOTES

Chapter Two

1. John C. Wright, "Atheist Morality, Part 1," http://johncwright. livejournal.com.

2. Lee Strobel, *The Case for Christ: A Journalist's Personal Investigation of the Evidence for Jesus* (Grand Rapids: Zondervan, 1998).

Chapter Five

1. See Augustine, *Confessions*, bk. 1, chap. 1, no. 1.

Chapter Seven

1. C.S. Lewis, *Mere Christianity* (New York: Touchstone, 1996), p. 39.

2. *The Diary of Virginia Woolf*, October 25, 1920, vol. 2 (Orlando, Fla.: Harcourt Brace, 1978), p. 72.

3. Lewis, p. 105.

4. Augustine, *Confessions*, bk. 10, chap. 27. Mary T. Clark, trans., *Augustine of Hippo: Selected Writings*, The Classics of Western Spirituality (Ramsey, N.J.: Paulist, 1984), p. 144.

Chapter Eight

1. Madeleine Delbrêl, *Nous autres, gens des rues* (Paris: Editions du seuil, 1966), p. 76.

2. Teresa of Avila, *Moradas del castillo interior*, "Segundas Moradas," in *Obras Completas* (Madrid: Biblioteca do Autores Cristianos, 1986), p. 482.

3. Cardinal John Henry Newman, "To be deep in history is to cease to be a Protestant," *An Essay on the Development of Christian Doctrine* (London: Longmans, Green, 1909), p. 8.

Chapter Ten

1. Communion and Liberation is pontifically recognized as a movement within the church. Its followers often refer to it affectionately as "the movement."

ABOUT THE AUTHOR

Rebecca Vitz Cherico is an adjunct professor at Villanova University. She is a member of the ecclesial movement Communion and Liberation and lives outside Philadelphia with her husband, Colin, and their four children.